Forth to Farne Way

North Berwick to Lindisfarne

John Henderson
and Jacquetta Megarry

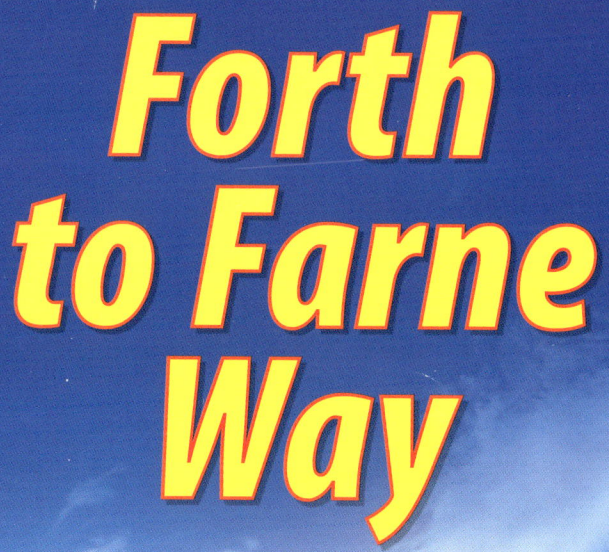

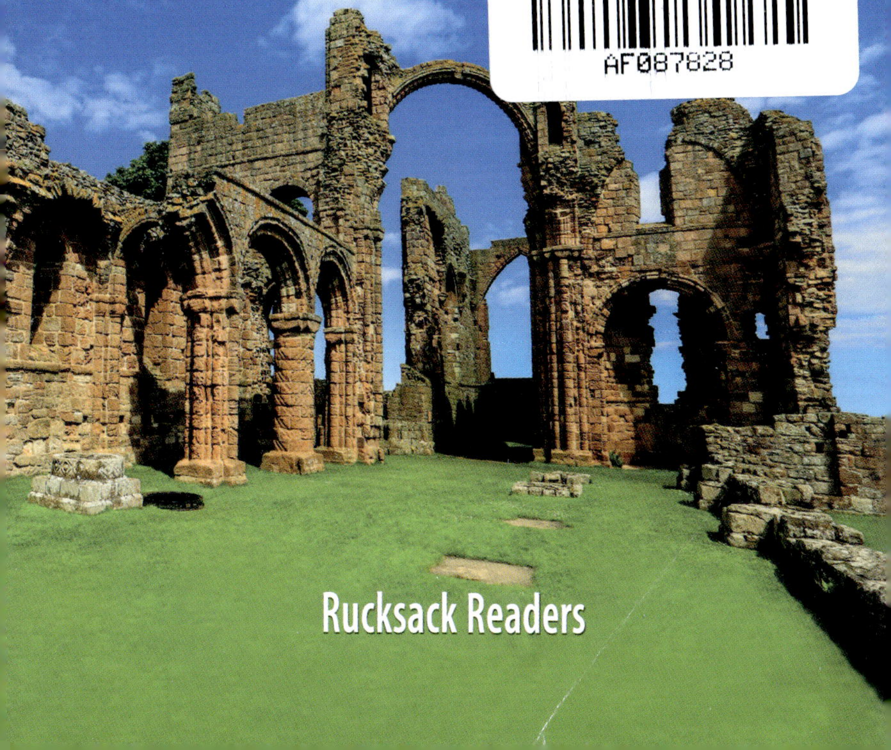

Rucksack Readers

Forth to Farne Way

First published in 2020 by Rucksack Readers
6 Old Church Lane, Edinburgh, EH15 3PX, UK
tel   +44/0 131 661 0262
email   info@rucsacs.com
web   ***www.rucsacs.com***

© text authors; photographs © licensors as listed on page 71.

The rights of John Henderson and Jacquetta Megarry to be identified as the authors of this work have been asserted by them.

All rights reserved. No part of this publication may be reproduced, stored in a retrieval system, or transmitted in any form or by any means, electronic, mechanical, photocopying, recording or otherwise, without prior permission in writing from the publisher and copyright holders.

ISBN 978-1-898481-96-6

British Library cataloguing in publication data: a catalogue record for this book is available from the British Library.

Designed in Scotland by Ian Clydesdale (*ian@workhorse.scot*)

Printed and bound in the UK by Short Run Press, Exeter on rainproof, biodegradable paper

Mapping is © Rucksack Readers and was created specially for this book by Lovell Johns. It contains Ordnance Survey data © Crown copyright and database rights 2020 with further material collected by the authors.

Publisher's note
All information was checked prior to publication. However, changes are inevitable: take local advice and look out for new waymarkers to augment other signage. Walkers are advised to check two websites for updates before setting out:
  www.forthtofarne.org
  www.rucsacs.com/books/f2f

The weather in this area is changeable, and some parts of the route run along exposed cliff-tops and through remote countryside. Do not rely on having mobile phone (cellphone) reception. You are responsible for your own safety, for ensuring that your clothing, food and equipment are suited to your needs and that your intended walk can safely be completed in daylight. The publisher accepts no liability for any ill-health, injury or loss arising directly or indirectly from reading this book.

Feedback is welcome and will be rewarded
All feedback will be followed up, and readers whose comments lead to changes will be entitled to claim a free copy of our next edition upon publication. Please send emails to **info@rucsacs.com**.

Contents

Introduction / Foreword — 4

1 Planning to walk the Way — 5
- Best time of year and weather — 6
- Which direction? — 7
- How long will it take? — 7
- The Pilgrim Way to Lindisfarne — 8
- Getting there and away — 9
- Accommodation and refreshments — 10
- Terrain and gradients — 10
- Navigation and waymarking — 12
- Responsible access — 13
- Livestock, walkers and dogs — 13
- Packing checklist — 14

2 Background information
- 2·1 Fourteen centuries of pilgrimage — 15
- 2·2 Geology and scenery — 18
- 2·3 Coastal communities — 21
- 2·4 Wildlife and habitats — 24

3 The Way in detail
- North Berwick — 28
- 3·1 North Berwick to Dunbar — 29
- 3·2 Dunbar to Cockburnspath — 39
- Cockburnspath — 45
- 3·3 Cockburnspath to St Abbs — 46
- 3·4 St Abbs to Berwick upon Tweed — 54
- Berwick upon Tweed — 62
- 3·5 Berwick upon Tweed to Lindisfarne — 64
- Holy Island of Lindisfarne — 69

6 Reference
- Useful websites, transport and travel — 70
- Further reading, maps, accommodation and credits — 71
- Index — 72

Foreword

Pilgrimage is an ancient tradition in all parts of the world. In Tibet, for hundreds of years pilgrims in their thousands from at least four different religions have made their ritual circuit of Mount Kailash, Tibet's Sacred Mountain. Nearer home in Ireland, from time immemorial even before the arrival of Christianity, thousands of pilgrims have regularly climbed to the summit of what is now called Croagh Patrick, Ireland's Holy Mountain.

Happily, pilgrimage is now becoming a very modern practice as well. Scotland is blessed with ancient pilgrim routes which are being revived and new ones which are being created. All benefit from our unique combination of glorious scenery and sites of historic significance. The Forth to Farne Way does just that.

Along the Way, you can imagine the future Pope Pius II walking barefoot through the snow to St Mary's Well at Whitekirk, in thanksgiving for surviving a tempestuous sea journey. And, on reaching the end of the route at the Holy Island of Lindisfarne, you can think of St Cuthbert spending the last years of his life there.

With its combination of exercise for the body, mind and soul, modern pilgrimage in Scotland is surely set to grow and flourish. On the Forth to Farne Way the steep climbs and long days will offer a physical challenge. The fascinating geology and coastal heritage will stimulate the mind; and the soul will be cheered by the pilgrim lives and religious buildings that are documented throughout this inspirational, informative and practical guide.

David Wilson
Lord Wilson of Tillyorn,
Patron of the Scottish Pilgrim Routes Forum

1 Planning to walk the Way

Welcome to a walk that may inspire you spiritually, as well as challenge you physically. An immense variety of terrain, scenery and experiences await you in your 70-mile journey from North Berwick to Lindisfarne. After a largely inland first section, the Forth to Farne Way clings closely to the coast from Dunbar onward, with brief detours inland to visit Cockburnspath and Coldingham Priory.

This is coastal walking at its finest, mainly on a mixture of beaches, clifftop and field-edge paths. The sounds, smells and sights of the sea are everywhere, as is the history of its coastal communities. You pass magnificent lighthouses, moving memorials to the fishing disaster of 1881 and several harbours – some disused, like Pettico Wick below, others still busy with boats for fishing and diving. If you eat fish and seafood, you may enjoy some locally caught harvest after a hard day's walk.

You walk on town pavements in North Berwick, Dunbar and Berwick upon Tweed – where the legacy of centuries of warfare is visible in the ramparts, bastions and town walls. But you will also experience the remoteness of deserted clifftops, rugged headlands and dramatic ravines, with the music of the waves and cries of the seabirds ringing in your ears. And it is difficult to imagine a more romantic finale than the Pilgrim Way, crossing the North Sea barefoot to the Holy Island of Lindisfarne.

How much experience do you need to take on this challenge enjoyably? Surprisingly, the answer may be little or none, as long as you take time to prepare and plan. Part 1 of this book is all about planning, and we offer advice to novice walkers on our website: see page 71.

Pettico Wick harbour, near St Abbs Head

Best time of year and weather

Most people will opt to walk the Forth to Farne Way in late spring, summer or early autumn. Wildflowers are at their best in late spring and summer, and birds are more active and visible during early spring and late autumn. Accommodation will also be more limited out of season, so the best times overall are generally from Easter to October.

Good Friday is an auspicious and popular day upon which to make the Pilgrim Way crossing to Lindisfarne, thanks to the Synod of Whitby: see the panel below. If you want to include the barefoot crossing in your itinerary (at any time of year), read page 8. You'll have to research tide times long before finalising your dates.

In theory, the Way could be walked at any time of year. It does not venture to high altitude and the major constraints on winter walking are short days, greater chance of wet, windy weather and sodden ground in the offroad sections. Unless you live at high latitude (about 56° N) you may not realise how short the daylight can become – fewer than eight hours in late December.

Finally, be aware that this stretch of coast is prone to sea fog (aka haar or sea fret), especially in summer months. It forms when warm moist air is chilled by the North Sea, causing condensation. Unless the land is warm and the sunshine strong, the fog may take a long time to burn off, especially if a sea breeze keeps sweeping more fog inland. It is not only damp and cooling, but also reduces visibility drastically; this can make navigation challenging. Banks of sea fog may begin and end abruptly.

Above: Lindisfarne Castle from the west
Below: As seen through sea fog

Tides at Easter
The Synod of Whitby was held in AD664: see page 16. It was convened to settle the correct date for Easter, agreed as the first Sunday after the first full moon after 20th March. A neat consequence of the Synod is that Easter pilgrims who arrive at Beal Sands on the morning of Good Friday will always find the tide is out, ready for their crossing of the Pilgrim Way.

Which direction?

We describe the route in the recommended southbound direction, with Lindisfarne as its culmination. It is of course possible to reverse this, and some walkers may have logistic reasons for ending their walk at North Berwick instead. Northbound walkers may experience the wind at their backs more often than southbound. However, we prefer to begin the route inland, then to follow increasingly rugged coastal scenery until the crossing to Lindisfarne and Holy Island itself make a fitting finale.

How long will it take?

We present the route in five sections, but most walkers will want to spend six or more days, and many will split the route differently. The ideal itinerary depends on your interest in detours, on the time you need to rest or contemplate, and on your fitness, travel arrangements and accommodation availability. The route is intended as a long and enjoyable walk, not as a test of endurance or speed.

Some will wish to complete the route in a single expedition, whilst others may split it into two or more excursions, using the excellent train and bus services that serve North Berwick, Dunbar and Berwick upon Tweed.

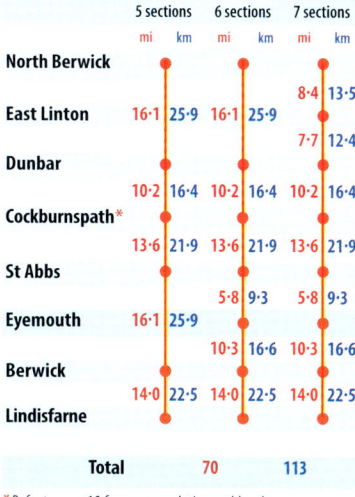

Table 1: the Way can be split in three ways

	5 sections		6 sections		7 sections	
	mi	km	mi	km	mi	km
North Berwick						
					8·4	13·5
East Linton	16·1	25·9	16·1	25·9		
					7·7	12·4
Dunbar						
	10·2	16·4	10·2	16·4	10·2	16·4
Cockburnspath*						
	13·6	21·9	13·6	21·9	13·6	21·9
St Abbs						
			5·8	9·3	5·8	9·3
Eyemouth	16·1	25·9				
			10·3	16·6	10·3	16·6
Berwick						
	14·0	22·5	14·0	22·5	14·0	22·5
Lindisfarne						
Total		70				113

*Refer to page 10 for accommodation problem here

Distances are shown in Table 1, in which you will see two sections that are over 16 miles/26 km – too long for a single day for many walkers even in the long days of summer. Splitting section 3·1 may require some support from a car or taxi driver in that public transport is scarce, and in 2020 there was only one B&B close to the route in East Linton. However it consists of easier, flatter walking than 3·4, and anyway the last few miles are around Dunbar to its parish church. If you stay near the western end of Dunbar you could postpone those miles to the start of your next day.

By contrast, section 3·4 has much more altitude gain and loss and also finer coastal scenery that you may wish to linger over. Happily, it also has intermediate places where accommodation is available, notably Coldingham (limited) and Eyemouth (with wider choice). So if you intend to split only one of the two longest sections, we suggest that you choose 3·4.

Another choice that will determine whether you need to add an extra night is how long you intend to spend on the tidal island of Lindisfarne, and which route you wish to take. Whilst it is just about possible to walk the 14 miles from Berwick to Lindisfarne Priory and, if tide and daylight permit, immediately turn around to return to the mainland on the same day, it would certainly be very challenging. Such a plan would demand extremely careful planning to fit two crossings within a tidal window, and would force you to use the car-busy causeway rather than the peaceful Pilgrim Way across the sands. And on many days the timing of tides and hours of daylight would make such a plan impossible.

In our view, having walked so far to such a special place, you should allow yourself time to enjoy it as a true island. If you want to arrive barefoot by the Pilgrim Way, you will need at least one overnight anyway. We recommend that you stay for two or more if possible. (Many B&Bs on Lindisfarne insist on two-night stays, especially at weekends.) Some may prefer an extended stay, whether to go into retreat, to watch the wildlife or to make repeated visits to Lindisfarne's many visitor attractions: see page 69.

The Pilgrim Way to Lindisfarne

Timing is crucial: plan your crossing long in advance. The tidal window varies in length and often falls at an inconvenient or unsafe time of day: don't attempt the crossing in failing light or stormy weather. Judge for yourself, and if in doubt, don't.

Aim to set off on a falling tide, and allow 75-90 minutes to complete the crossing safely and calmly. If you arrive too early, you could detour (1·4 km each way) to the Barn at Beal for refreshments, but if you arrive too late, you'll have to use the causeway – or perhaps not cross at all.

The causeway 'safe' period varies in length from 5¼ hours to over 9 hours, but the safe window for the lower, more time-consuming Pilgrim Way is 3-4 hours shorter. At a time of extreme tides, therefore, you may have very little leeway about your start time. The goal is to complete your crossing by the time the tide turns, which is the midpoint of the advertised causeway safe crossing period.

Don't wear walking shoes: sticky mud and salt water will ruin them. We recommend bare feet with the option of crocs or waterproof sandals for short rough bits, including tarmac at the start and finish. If possible, carry a small towel to dry your feet and legs, and perhaps also binoculars if you are interested in seabirds and other wildlife.

Most of the terrain is firm sand, with mostly shallow sea water lying over firm sand; some short sections have rough vegetation and foot-sucking mud. Generally follow the line of wooden poles but don't be afraid to deviate slightly to avoid the occasional quagmire.

Take your time to savour this unique experience, every now and then making a 360° turn to drink in the sights and sounds of the North Sea.

West from Lindisfarne across the Pilgrim Way

Getting there and away

Table 2: Distances and fastest journey times between selected places

	miles	km	by bus	by train	by car
Edinburgh - London	375	605	9h 20m	4 h 20m	7h
Edinburgh - North Berwick	25	40	1h 15m	25m	35m
Edinburgh - Dunbar	30	48	1h 5m	20m	45m
Edinburgh - Berwick	60	96	1h 20m	40m	1h
Berwick - Lindisfarne*	15	24	35m**	–	30m
Berwick - Newcastle	65	105	1h 40m	45m	1h 15m
Berwick - London	340	550	8h 10m	3h 40m	6h

* access to Lindisfarne depends on the tidal window; when causeway traffic is heavy, journeys take much longer
** Borders Buses 477 via Beal but very infrequent – in 2020 about twice a week

Visitors from afar may wish to use Edinburgh airport, which is about 8 miles (13 km) west of the city centre with transfer options by tram, train, bus and taxi. There are frequent flights from London, but once you allow time for airport transfers and security, you may find that the train is no slower and is likely more comfortable.

The table above shows fastest journey times as of 2020 with no allowance for traffic or fuel stops for car journeys. Distances are rounded: in some cases road and rail distances differ slightly.

From Edinburgh, it is fairly quick to reach North Berwick by East Coast Buses (X5 and 124) but faster by train. There is also a frequent X7 service to Dunbar. A few London trains stop at Dunbar on the East Coast mainline en route for Edinburgh.

Borders Buses has a stopping service 253 from Edinburgh to Berwick that includes East Linton, Dunbar, Cockburnspath, Eyemouth and Burnmouth. In 2020 there were seven buses on weekdays. It also runs the twice-weekly 477 from Berwick to Lindisfarne. Eve Coaches has a useful route 120 that plies between Dunbar and North Berwick via East Linton and Whitekirk, in 2020 about seven times daily (not Sundays). See page 70 for contact details for transport providers: **check for updates** before relying on any of them.

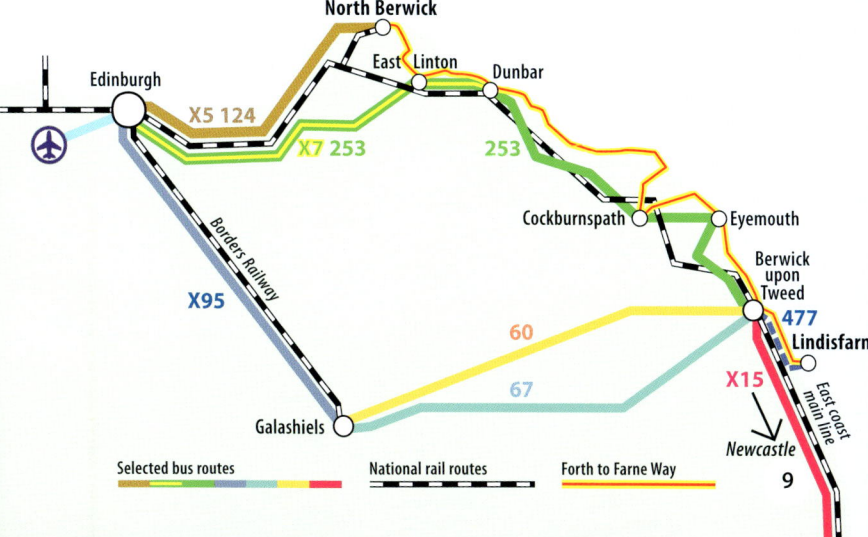

Accommodation and refreshments

Many walkers seek a hot evening meal and a soft bed after a hard day's walking. With this in mind, we have split the route in the expectation that you will probably wish to overnight in each of North Berwick, Dunbar, St Abbs, Berwick and Lindisfarne. Table 3 shows where you can find accommodation and refreshments, or at least where you could in 2020. The fallout from the Covid 19 pandemic may mean that some or many such options close and may not reopen. Check carefully before making plans.

A problem exists for anybody seeking a bed near the tiny village of Cockburnspath. Unless there is space at The Ramparts, a small B&B on the A1 near Dunglass, you would need help with transport to somewhere that has accommodation, or perhaps to spend two nights in Dunbar and get transport back to Dunbar from Cockburnspath, returning to the Way next morning. Check the links given on page 71 for any updates.

As of 2020, there were no hostels or other cheap beds except in Berwick and near Beal, so the only alternative is wild camping. This is legal in Scotland provided that it is done responsibly: see the panel about SOAC on page 13.

Refreshments are easier to manage: there are shops selling food of some kind in most places, and the main overnight stops have a range of pubs, cafés and take-aways. If your dietary needs are specialist, you may need to carry some supplies, but if you have a hearty breakfast and a good evening meal you may not need to carry much extra food. However, you should always carry plenty of drinking water for the day's walk, unless you rely on purifying tablets or filters.

Table 3: Facilities along the Way
These facilities existed in 2020, but after the pandemic some may not reopen in 2021; check before relying on them.

		B&B / hotel	hostel	pub / café	shop (food)
3·1	North Berwick	✓		✓	✓
	East Linton	✓			
3·2	Dunbar	✓		✓	✓
3·3	Cockburnspath				✓
	Pease Bay			✓	✓
3·4	St Abbs	✓		✓	✓
	Coldingham	✓		✓	✓
	Eyemouth	✓		✓	✓
	Burnmouth			✓	
3·5	Berwick upon Tweed	✓	✓	✓	✓

Terrain and gradients

The Way runs over a wide variety of surfaces, ranging from sandy and stony beaches through grassy footpaths and farm tracks to tarmac roads and pavements. The photos give some idea of the range of surfaces, but be aware that rainfall (before and around the time that you walk) also affects terrain. The state of the tide can transform beach walking, and firm damp sand is much easier to walk on than deep dry sand: pick your route accordingly.

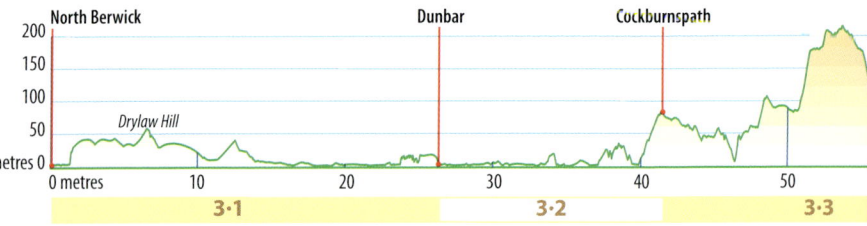

Some sections of the route have a number of gates and stiles, notably 3·4, and you may be surprised by how much these small obstacles reduce your average speed. They also may present challenges if you are walking with a dog. Even flights of steps and footbridges may slow you more than you expect. Most of the paths are fairly well-drained, but your footwear still needs to be waterproof for walking in the rain and through long wet grass.

The route is generally low-level, reaching its highest point of 210 m near Dowlaw Road in section 3·3. Do not fall into the trap of assuming that this makes for easy walking. There are many undulations in section 3·3 and the first half of 3·4 – with steep slopes in places, occasionally very steep. The flattest, easiest walking is in 3·1, 3·2 and 3·5 where you will find your stride more easily and eat the miles faster. However the Pilgrim Way, which is mostly at or below sea level and very flat indeed, makes for slow going for reasons explained on page 8.

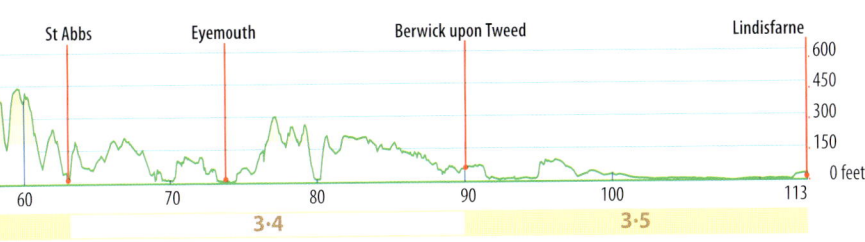

Navigation and waymarking

The mapping in Part 3 is detailed and closely linked with the route description: if you follow directions carefully, navigation should be straightforward. Note that north does not point up the page but is rotated through 50°. Each page carries a km grid that reminds you of this rotation. The route line has mileage indicators that are cumulative from North Berwick.

From 2021 the plan is to introduce some dedicated F2F waymarking: see the imprint page. Meanwhile we identify various signs for existing routes which help the walker, and in Part 3 we offer general advice at the start of each section. However, there are some places where there is no sign, or where you follow a sign for an unnamed footpath or numbered cycle route.

Also, some waymarks show subtle differences: for example, the John Muir Way not only uses different signs for walkers and cyclists, but also overlaps with a previous, shorter John Muir Way which had a different logo (an encircled butterfly). You will see this in places en route to Dunbar, where the more recent John Muir Way officially ends. Beyond it, a section was rebranded in 2014 as the John Muir Link whose signs still carry the butterfly.

Leaving Cockburnspath you need to follow Southern Upland Way signs at first, so look for the thistle-in-hexagon, at first on its own, then joined by the Berwickshire Coastal Path (BCP) blue disc with a white wave. Note that the BCP

is sometime signed simply as 'Coastal Path' inscribed on a fingerpost and sometimes by the blue disc (in places very faded). The disc may be supported by yellow arrows to confirm direction.

In Eyemouth look for green Coastal footpath signs which soon give way to blue BCP discs with a sprinkling of Smugglers' Trail and Cllifftop Footpath fingerposts.

South of the border, the Northumberland Coast Path is often signed as 'Coast Path', usually with a curved blue N. This was the logo of the North Sea Trail, an EU-funded project to improve walking trails in seven countries around the North Sea. The trail is partly shared with Cycle Route 1 and the Sandstone Way.

Responsible access

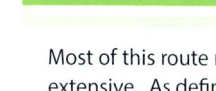 

Enjoy Scotland's outdoors responsibly
- take responsibility for your own actions
- respect the interests of other people
- care for the environment.

Most of this route runs through Scotland, where access rights for walkers are extensive. As defined by the Scottish Outdoor Access Code, everybody has the statutory right to take access to land, including that which is privately owned, for recreational purposes – provided only that those rights are exercised responsibly.

There are of course some exceptions, such as gardens, farmyards and fields under cultivation; however, landowners are encouraged to provide viable paths around field edges. See the panel and *outdooraccess-scotland.scot* for explicit and practical guidance.

Wild camping is allowed under SOAC provided it is done responsibly, but it does involve carrying much heavier loads and is not for the faint-hearted. There are very few campsites with facilities anywhere near the Way, although there are many caravan parks.

Once you cross the border into England (at mile 52·1) the position changes. England has four categories of public rights of way: footpaths (walkers only), bridleways (walkers, horseriders and cyclists) and two kinds of byway – *restricted* or *BOAT*. On this route, you'll see signs for 'restricted byway' – on which motorised vehicles are not allowed, as opposed to a 'byway open to all traffic' (BOAT) on which they are.

Rights of way are marked on Ordnance Survey and other maps, and recent maps also show areas of Access Land that allow walkers to leave paths and roam, under agreements reached with the landowners. Restrictions are explained at *www.openaccess.gov.uk*. In summary, in England you have no automatic right to walk over, let alone camp upon, privately owned land. Be guided by the 2020 version of the Countryside Code.

Countryside Code, England
Respect other people
- Consider the local community and other people enjoying the outdoors
- Park carefully so access to gateways and driveways is clear
- Leave gates and property as you find them
- Follow paths but give way to others where it's narrow

Protect the natural environment
- Leave no trace of your visit, take all your litter home
- Don't have BBQs or fires
- Keep dogs under effective control
- Dog poo - bag it and bin it

Enjoy the outdoors
- Plan ahead, check what facilities are open, be prepared
- Follow advice and local signs and obey social distancing measures

Livestock, walkers and dogs

Much of the Way passes through farmland with livestock. There may be cattle or sheep near the path or even standing or lying across it. Approach cattle with caution, especially if there are calves around. Most difficulties can be avoided by giving them a wide berth, staying alert to their body language and never approaching pregnant animals, let alone those with young.

If you walk with a dog, it must be under close control, and preferably on a lead. During lambing time (between March and June) your dog will be unwelcome in any fields with sheep. During the same season birds may be nesting on the ground, and again dogs must be under very close control. If cattle react aggressively to your dog, immediately let go of it and take the safest route out of the field.

Packing checklist

What you need to bring with you depends on your personal needs, on your itinerary and also on the season and likely weather: see page 71 for forecasts. If you are tackling the Way in sections, or if you have access to a support vehicle or baggage transfer at any time, you may not need to carry much overnight gear. If you are carrying everything for yourself, be aware that every kilogram counts. A heavy rucksack will not only make harder work out of stiles and steep slopes, but also will compromise your balance on an exposed clifftop. Travel light so as to enjoy your walk to the full.

Experienced walkers will already know what they habitually need, and may differ about what is essential and desirable. Novices may find the following checklist helpful:

Essential
- rucksack (minimum 30 litres)
- waterproof rucksack cover or liner
- comfortable, waterproof walking boots
- specialist walking socks (and spares)
- waterproof jacket & over-trousers
- clothing in layers (trousers, tops, jacket)
- hat – for warmth or sun protection
- this guidebook and a compass
- water carrier and enough drinking water (or a filtration system)
- food as needed between supply points
- whistle and torch to attract attention in case of accident
- toiletries and overnight necessities
- first aid kit including blister treatment
- insect repellent, sun protection (summer)
- cash, with credit/debit cards as back up.

Desirable
- gaiters (protect against ticks, wetness and mud)
- walking pole(s)
- gloves
- bin bags (useful for wet clothing and to keep other things dry)
- camera, charger/spare batteries, memory cards
- binoculars (for spotting wildlife)
- notebook & pen
- spare shoes (e.g. crocs or sandals)
- toilet tissue (biodegradable)
- towel if camping or hostelling
- mobile phone (cellphone) and charger.

A mobile phone (cellphone) is useful for making arrangements but reception is patchy. **Don't rely on a mobile for emergencies.**

Camping

If you are camping you need much more gear, including a tent, sleeping gear, camping stove, fuel and cooking utensils, food and a larger rucksack (e.g. 50-80 litres). Camping gear could add 5 to 10 kg to its weight, or even more. Previous experience is advisable. NB Camping is not permitted anywhere on Lindisfarne, and elsewhere in England you may camp only with permission from the relevant landowner.

2·1 Fourteen centuries of pilgrimage

The Forth to Farne Way follows a large part of the old established pilgrim route linking St Andrews with the Holy Island of Lindisfarne. From the early 12th century this route was travelled in both directions by pilgrims. The original start was from St Andrews to Earlsferry in Fife, then it crossed the Firth of Forth to North Berwick. That is where the Forth to Farne Way picks up the old route and follows it to Lindisfarne.

All along this Way there are links to early Christian saints and to historic nunneries, priories, churches, pilgrim hostels and holy wells. This route was walked by a constant flow of medieval pilgrims, including monks, nuns and saints. The pilgrimage tradition was supported by religious communities and pilgrim hostels, some of which had royal funding.

An important visit for the medieval pilgrim was Whitekirk, the site of a 15th century church, holy well and of pilgrim hostels established by King James I. Sadly the holy well and hostels no longer exist, but the church is still in active use. A notable visitor in 1435 was Aeneas Silvius Piccolomini. He arrived having promised the Virgin Mary to walk barefoot to her nearest shrine if she delivered him safely from a stormy sea passage. Upon arrival at Dunbar he must have been dismayed to discover that this involved a barefoot walk of over ten miles through the snow. Afterwards he suffered badly from painful feet, which he attributed to this episode. Many years later he became Pope Pius II, reigning from 1458-64.

This first part of the Way runs through East Lothian, where St Baldred, the 'Apostle of the Lothians', was active in the 8th century. Baldred came from the monastic community of Lindisfarne to spread the Christian message. He was also known as 'Baldred of the Bass' because he built a chapel and hermitage on the Bass Rock, where he made frequent retreats. He founded a monastery at Tyninghame and a church at East Linton – Preston Kirk, see page 33. The Way passes St Baldred's Well nearby: in the 13th century this provided water to the nearby monastery, and it continued to supply the village into the 20th century.

The Bass Rock, where St Baldred made his retreats

A recommended visit near Cockburnspath is Dunglass Collegiate Church, a remarkably intact medieval example of its kind, with superbly carved stonework: see pages 43 and 44 The original nave and choir were enhanced in the 16th century with transepts and a tower. After a period of decay and partial restoration, it was taken over by Historic Environment Scotland: see page 70. Nearby, the Way visits the pre-Reformation Cockburnspath Parish Church, featured on page 45.

Andrew Usher's Northfield House: see page 52

The spread of Christianity in Northumbria (which then extended to North Berwick) was largely the work of two children of its pagan King Aethelfrith – Ebba and Oswald. After Aethelfrith was killed in AD 616, his family took refuge in Iona where they were converted by followers of St Columba. Both were key figures in spreading the Celtic version of Christianity throughout the area, and until the Synod of Whitby (AD 664) Northumbria adhered to this, rather than the Roman interpretation. Both Ebba and Oswald were later made saints, and Oswald also became King of Northumbria.

Ebba's name is sometimes spelled Abb or Aebba, and she lived in the 7th century. In AD 695 Ebba set up separate communities of monks and nuns, and later a church, on Kirk Hill: see page 52. Shortly after Ebba's death, St Abb's Kirk was destroyed by fire, and a church was built at Coldingham, just a couple of miles inland.

Coldingham Priory was founded by Edgar King of Scots in 1098 AD and at first was home to 30 Benedictine monks from Durham. It was well endowed by Edgar and attracted many gifts and privileges from later Scottish kings and other donors, becoming one of Scotland's wealthiest and most important religious sites. In its heyday, it was the hub of an empire built on land ownership, with income from timber sales and the export of wool.

Head of St Ebba

After the original church was destroyed by King John of England in 1216, a larger and more splendid church replaced it on the same site. Various attacks did further damage, culminating in Oliver Cromwell's siege of 1650 which destroyed all but the north and east walls of the choir. These were later incorporated into the church that you see today, which explains the contrast between their ornamental arches and the very plain south and west walls. The building is well used as the local parish church, and welcomes modern pilgrims.

Looking east, Coldingham Priory church

The Way ends at Lindisfarne Priory, established in AD 635 by Aidan who was its first bishop and later was canonised. He had been invited by Oswald, now King of Northumbria, to come from Iona to spread the Christian message. About this time another monastic community was established at Old Melrose, where St Boisil and St Cuthbert first became Priors before moving to Lindisfarne. The original monastic community had to flee the Viking invasion of AD 793, but monks returned to the island later and re-established the priory which still stands as a partial ruin. For visit information, see page 70.

Lindisfarne Priory has strong links with St Cuthbert, who was its third Prior and bishop: see page 69. However his body was moved for safety and was finally buried at Durham Cathedral. When it was opened in 1827, they found a beautiful cross of gold studded with garnets around his neck.

Lindisfarne has remained a focus of pilgrimage over the centuries, and became the fitting destination of both St Cuthbert's and St Oswald's Ways. They are now joined by the Forth to Farne Way, which celebrates the resurgence of pilgrimage walking in the 21st century.

St Cuthbert's Cross

St Aidan facing Lindisfarne Priory

2·2 Geology and scenery

Geology defines the scenery of the Way. Whilst no geological knowledge is essential to enjoying your walk, a basic understanding of the rock types and their origins will enhance your experience. The landscape that you walk through reveals traces of the processes that created it.

The oldest rocks are sedimentary, deposited on the sea bed about 440-420 million years ago (mya) – grey mudstones and siltstones. About 350-320 mya central Scotland was located south of the equator and its lowlands were occupied by tropical seas. Vast deposits of animal shells and skeletons were laid down, which eventually turned into limestone.

The processes of depositing sediment and forming these rocks continued for about another 100 million years. Two periods of volcanic activity (about 400 and 345 mya) produced hard, igneous rocks such as *dolerite* and *andesite*: see page 20. These occur both as large outcrops and as intrusions into other rocks. Below we list selected places on the Way where geology is most visible.

Near the mouth of the Brox Burn (mile 17·2) is a good example of a raised beach – sand and shingle deposits that originated as a beach at tide level. Later the land rose when it was released from the weight of melting glaciers, and the sea level fell – leaving the beach high and dry, without water or waves.

From about mile 19, Barns Ness Coast is a Site of Special Scientific Interest, valued for its variety of rock types and their history, and also for the plants that flourish around them. The short walk from White Sands Bay to Barns Ness lighthouse lets you see the most extensive limestone outcrops in central Scotland, with many other sedimentary rocks such as sandstone, mudstone and coal, and plenty of fossils. Information boards along the Catcraig Geology Trail here document nine different kinds of limestone.

You can see human exploitation of limestone: in the 18th century farmers built lime kilns in which limestone and coal were burned to create fertiliser to improve yield in their crops. More recently came a quarry and cement works. To view fossils and limestones on the foreshore, it's ideal to visit at low tide.

The beaches along this coastline are composed of shingle (pebbles) and sand, as are the sand dunes further inland which are colonised with marram and other grasses.

Shingle beach south-east of Barns Ness

Mire Loch seen from the Way

Further on, Siccar Point is a short detour from the Way (mile 29·7). Its discovery by James Hutton was a major event in the history of geology: see page 47.

Faults form when activity deep in the earth's crust causes a fracture between two blocks of rock so that the blocks move relative to each other. Faults are visible around Barns Ness Coast, and also, much further east, at St Abb's Head.

You cross the St Abb's Head fault at mile 37·8 – its line revealed by the manmade Mire Loch. This marshy area hollowed out by glacial meltwater was dammed in 1900 to create a loch for fishing and other sports.

To its west, even older sedimentary rocks – dark sandstones called greywacke – have been squeezed into tight folds. At about 430 mya they are the oldest rocks in the area. They make up most of Scotland's Southern Uplands.

Folded greywacke west of Pettico Wick

The steep promontories around St Abb's Head are made of igneous rocks, formed in the magma chamber 360-350 mya. These include dark dolerite, formed from slow-cooling lava and containing visible mineral crystals. It contrasts with paler pink/grey andesite, formed from fast-cooling lava with crystals that are tiny, invisible to the naked eye. All around these headlands, the scenery is rugged, with rocky outcrops, sea arches and pinnacles.

Around Eyemouth Fort (mile 45) you'll see another sedimentary rock: old red sandstone. Formed of river deposits as 'recently' as 358 mya, its red colour comes from traces of iron oxide.

Rocky pinnacles near St Abbs (mile 39·4)

South of Eyemouth, you walk past the golf course up to the high cliffs around Blaikie Heugh (103 m). The views are spectacular, with fine examples of folded sedimentary strata formed about 440-420 mya.

The Northumberland coast is similar in origins to Berwickshire. The main rock types are sedimentary – limestones, sandstones and shales. Rugged platforms of igneous (volcanic) rock reach out into the sea from the base of softer cliffs, forming reefs and headlands. It is the latter that explains the origins of the Farne Islands, including the Way's destination of Lindisfarne.

Eyemouth Fort headland

Folded strata of sedimentary rock (mile 47)

2·3 Coastal communities

'Widows and Bairns' bronzes, St Abbs

Fishing

Fishing is the lifeblood of the villages on this stretch of coastline, and the shared experience of the sea's harvest, and of its dangers, has built a strong sense of community. In the era before technological aids to weather forecasting and navigation were developed, fishing was much more dangerous than today.

Scotland's worst fishing disaster befell boats from four local harbours (Cove, St Abbs, Eyemouth and Burnmouth) on Black Friday in October 1881. Impatient after a week of being confined to port, the fleet went to sea despite the barometer being ominously low. Some skippers were dubious, but tradition dictated that if one boat went out, they all did. The morning appeared calm but before long, a sudden hurricane blew up.

The storm overpowered 19 fishing boats, and 189 local fishermen were drowned, of whom 129 were from Eyemouth. Some boats were smashed on the rocks near the shore, helplessly watched from the land by their families. Other boats chose to run before the storm and were driven as far as Norway. After the disaster, many survivors moved away, and the population did not recover until 1971.

The huge Eyemouth Tapestry records the events and names in nearly 1 million stitches. It took 24 local women two years to complete for the 1981 centenary, and it can be viewed in the museum: see page 57. Much later, in 2016 Jill Watson's bronze statues 'Widows and Bairns' were unveiled to commemorate the 93 widows and 267 fatherless children of the disaster. The Way passes three of the four bronzes – to the right of the St Abbs Visitor Centre, on Eyemouth's promenade (see page 57) and at Burnmouth Harbour (see page 59). Each group represents in detail the bereaved families from each village.

The Eyemouth Tapestry

Eyemouth is the largest and oldest of these fishing ports. Active since the 13th century, its main growth came later, in the 19th century. By 1900 it was home to about 50 boats, taking herring from May to October and cod, haddock and whiting in winter. Supporting trades such as coopering, net mending and rope making all flourished. Its traditional layout of narrow streets and alleys give shelter from the sea and help to conceal smuggling. The harbour was improved in 1890 (see the panel on page 53) and again in 1965. In 1997 conversion to a deep water port brought a new lease of life. Eyemouth is still a working fishing port, concentrating on shellfish.

The small St Abbs fleet also brings in shellfish, and the clear waters around the headland make for as many dive boats as fishing boats. The harbour was a major supplier to Coldingham Priory in its heyday, with fishermen carrying their catch up the Creel Road: see page 54. Indeed the village's name was changed from Coldingham Shore to St Abbs only in the 1890s. Long ago, there was a salmon fishing station at nearby Pettico Wick, and you can still see the slipway at its eastern end.

Burnmouth had its fishing harbour built in the 1830s, and later it was extended both in 1879 and 1959. The village is in four parts scattered around a steep valley formed by a burn that cut through the 90-metre cliffs. Upper Burnmouth lies at the level of the clifftop with the A1 road, mainline railway and the First and Last pub. From there, the Way descends steeply to the lower village, focused on its harbours but extending to Cowdrait on a narrow road squeezed between the cliffs and the sea.

Lighthouses

Safety at sea still depends on lighthouses in key locations, and the Way passes two very fine examples. The 37 m-high Barns Ness light was completed in 1901 by David A Stevenson and his brother Charles. Two keepers resided there until 1966 when it was electrified, then one keeper stayed on until 1986 when it was automated. It closed in 2005 and later was sold: see page 40 for its photo.

Following the sinking of the Martello in 1857, St Abbs installed a lighthouse. Designed and built by brothers David and Thomas Stevenson, it made brilliant use of the cliffs to place its platform 68 metres above sea level. The lighthouse stands only 9 metres tall, to reduce the risk of sea fog obscuring its light. Its Fresnel lens uses polished crystal glass set into a bronze lattice. Long before there was access by road, supplies for the three keepers were landed at Pettico Wick to its west. The fog siren, installed in 1876 and driven by hot air engines, was the first in Scotland, and sounded until 1987.

St Abbs lighthouse

Lindisfarne has no lighthouses, but its historic navigation aids are elegant and visible. At Emmanuel Head off the island's north-east corner, a white brick pyramid 10 m tall was built in 1810 to identify the safe entrance to deep water. It may have been the first daymark on mainland Britain. To the south, two tall obelisks were installed in about 1820-40 on Guile Point to give seafarers the correct heading by which to approach. Afterwards, the Heugh Hill beacon and St Mary's church tower were aligned to allow safe entrance to the harbour. Before modern electronic aids, these daytime markers were real life-savers.

Obelisks at Guile Point

Lifeboats and the RNLI

Lifeboats were in service along the coast from the early 19th century, the first based at Dunbar in 1808. The Royal National Lifeboat Institution (as it is now called) was founded in London in 1824. Berwick upon Tweed's lifeboat followed nine years later. Lifeboat stations were set up at North Berwick (1869) and Eyemouth (1876) under the auspices of the RNLI.

The St Abbs station arrived much later in 1911, after a Danish ship was wrecked nearby. After a review of lifeboat services, even though more than 330 lives had been saved, the RNLI closed the station in 2011, claiming that coverage was better provided by Eyemouth. However, the St Abbs community was unconvinced and set about raising funds. Assisted by a substantial private donation, their campaign was successful and a new independent boat was launched in 2016.

Smuggling

Smuggling was a part of coastal life until well into the 19th century. John Nisbet was a notorious smuggler who worked as an apparently respectable merchant in Eyemouth. He had architect John Adam design the impressive Gunsgreen House in 1753: see page 58. Its tunnels allowed sea access and its cellars stored tea, tobacco and brandy that he imported illicitly. His Nisbet Tower gave him useful advance warning of unwelcome visits from customs officers.

Eventually Nisbet was bankrupted after a court case brought by a rival, who moved into Gunsgreen House. After it had became derelict in 1998, it was rescued by a local charitable trust which now runs it as a Smugglers Museum. For visit information, go to ***www.gunsgreenhouse.org***.

Nisbet Tower

2·4 Wildlife and habitats

Brown hare

Whilst most of the Way runs along the North Sea coast, it visits three other habitat types. Its first 14 miles run inland, through farmland and on quiet roads with hedgerows, with some riverside and estuary habitats east of East Linton (mile 8·4). The Way also briefly visits patches of woodland in wooded steep valleys known as deans. It also runs through two National Nature Reserves (NNRs) – St Abb's Head and Lindisfarne.

Below we focus on farmland and coast, ending with a page about the wildflowers and colourful insects that feed on them. Butterflies are a special feature of this route, and a good reason to walk it in late spring or summer.

Farmland

Painted lady

Recent environmental schemes have encouraged farmers to sustain more biodiversity around farmland. When walking field-edge paths, even around arable crops, look for wildflowers and small birds and perhaps a brown hare scurrying away. In summer you may be thrilled by the melodious song of the skylark. Like many other small birds, they feed on seeds and insects.

Hedgerows host a range of colourful plants – gorse, hawthorn, dog rose and bramble – whose flowers and fruits attract small birds such as wrens and yellowhammers. They also provide vital shelter for small mammals such as bats, wood mice, voles, hedgehogs and hares.

The Way passes some short stretches of freshwater: it runs beside the River Tyne for 2 miles. This is a good place to see the dipper – a white-chested dark brown bird with brilliant fishing skills – and wagtails, both pied and grey. If you are very lucky, you might spot the turquoise flash of a dashing kingfisher.

Mire Loch (see page 51) lies within St Abb's Head NNR. Its freshwater supports eels, sticklebacks, frogs and toads, and also swans and ducks. The insect and bird life here is remarkable too, with damselflies and butterflies, yellowhammers and the tiny goldcrest. Weighing only 6 grams, this is one of Britain's tiniest birds. In autumn, huge numbers arrive on the east coast to escape the Scandinavian winter, but they can be spotted year-round.

Goldcrest

Coast

Before embarking on the Way, consider visiting North Berwick's offshore islands which are notable for their bird life and accessible by boat in season. The Bass Rock (see

Gannet

page 15) hosts over 150,000 gannets, the largest colony north of the equator. Gannets fly to heights of 30 metres, then fold their wings and dive-bomb their prey at speeds of over 50 mph (80 kph). The Isle of May is famous for its wide range of seabirds including guillemots, razorbills, kittiwakes, shags, eiders, fulmars and terns and, in season, you gain close views of its 100,000 puffins. Over 2000 grey seal pups are born here every autumn. To discover boat trip options, visit **www.seabird.org**.

Oystercatchers

From Dunbar to Lindisfarne, the Way never strays far from the North Sea coast, which supports a wide range of wildlife both offshore and inland. The Tyne estuary is a haven for coastal birds such as oystercatchers, easily recognised by their plumage and loud piercing call. Long-legged waders feed on the mudflats, including redshanks, greenshanks and bar-tailed godwits.

Much of the Way runs along clifftop paths where you will see many kinds of gull soaring, or even a bird of prey such as a kestrel or sparrowhawk hunting on the cliffs. If you are lucky, you may even glimpse a peregrine,

Redshank

the most powerful and agile falcon. It preys on pigeons and other smallish birds that it catches 'on the wing'. It is by far the fastest bird in the world, achieving speeds of well over 180 mph (290 kph). It needs special baffles in its nostrils so it can still breathe at such speeds.

Peregrine

Grey seal (female)

Britain's coast is home to 40% of the world's population of Atlantic grey seals, which are larger, and in this area more common, than the common (harbour) seal. If you can see their heads, the differences are obvious: the grey has a flatter head with a Roman nose, whilst the common seal's head is rounded with V-shaped nostrils. Your best chance to view them is where they haul out on Lindisfarne's shores. Binoculars are useful: please don't disturb them by approaching closely.

Lindisfarne's National Nature Reserve has a huge area of dunes, saltmarsh and mudflats. The sand, once stabilised by marram and other grasses, supports a wide range of plants including 11 species of orchid. Out of season, the mudflats provide food to massive flocks of Arctic waterfowl, including 40% of the world's light-bellied brent geese. Other visitors include pink-footed geese, wigeons, plovers and bar-tailed godwits. Look out (and listen) for the eider, Britain's heaviest and fastest duck, which feasts on shellfish, notably mussels. St Cuthbert is said to have tamed and protected these seaducks, known locally as the Cuddy duck.

Bar-tailed godwits

Eider duck (male)

Marram grass

Wildflowers and insects

The Way begins in East Lothian, whose county flower is viper's bugloss. It continues through Berwickshire, the land of the rock rose. And it ends in Northumberland, which identifies with the bloody cranesbill. These three county flowers are celebrated for their attractiveness, not just to humans but also to pollinators. Viper's bugloss is a member of the borage family, its unusual name coming from bugloss – Greek for rough texture– and viper – after the forked tongue of its stamen.

Pollinators, especially butterflies such as painted lady and large skipper, love viper's bugloss, which also attracts bumblebees. The rock rose behaves like a sunflower: its petals open in sunshine and close at night. It also provides nectar for bees, and has an important role in butterfly conservation. Its leaves are the only food source for the caterpillars of the rare northern brown argus. The fenced area near St Abb's Head (mile 38·5) excludes sheep from nibbling the rock rose for this very reason.

Bloody cranesbill is rich in nectar and popular with butterflies and bees, especially bumblebees. A member of the geranium family, its leaves darken in autumn, turning blood-brown, while the shape of its seed capsule resembles a crane's bill.

Many other colourful insects thrive along the Way, including ladybirds, damselflies and dragonflies, but butterflies are some of the easiest to spot and recognise.

Viper's bugloss

Rock rose

Bloody cranesbill

Northern brown argus

3 North Berwick

North Berwick is a small town (population about 6600) over 40 miles north-west of its better-known cousin Berwick upon Tweed, perched on a headland jutting north into the Firth of Forth. Its fine natural harbour was a popular departure point for pilgrims from all over Scotland on their way across the Forth to St Andrews in Fife. They would have first visited St Andrew's Auld Kirk, where the Way begins, and some would have stayed in the nunnery nearby before the crossing.

North Berwick flourished in the Middle Ages and the chuch was expanded, but much of its building collapsed into the sea in the 17th century. You can explore its ruined walls and read its history from a display inside the porch.

Your travel arrangements may require an overnight in North Berwick, especially if you intend to complete the entire section to Dunbar next day. Anyway you should consider planning time to explore the town or to climb North Berwick Law (187 m). The Scottish Seabird Centre is an award-winning attraction adjacent to the Auld Kirk, with excellent displays, simulations and audiovisual shows. It also offers (in season) boat trips to the Bass Rock and Isle of May: www.seabird.org.

Across the ruins of the Auld Kirk to the Scottish Seabird Centre

The Isle of May is known as the 'jewel of the Forth' and (in season) a landing trip is an amazing experience, not only for its wildlife but also because of its very early Christian legacy. St Ethernan (St Adrian) came here as a missionary in about AD 840, but he and his fellow Christains were pursued by the Danes and massacred on the island in AD 875. Whether boats can land on the May depends on tides and weather, so planning is required.

West over Milsey Bay to North Berwick

3·1 North Berwick to Dunbar

31	34	35	38

Distance 16·1 miles 25·9 km
Terrain minor roads, beach, grassy paths, farm tracks and pavement
Grade mainly level or gently undulating
Food and drink North Berwick, East Linton, Dunbar (wide range)
Side-trip John Muir's birthplace, Dunbar
Summary inland walking through farmland, woodland and riverside/estuary; culminates in the clifftop approach to Dunbar

mile 0 — North Berwick — 7·4 — 4·6 Whitekirk — 6·1 — 3·8 East Linton — 5·0 — 3·1 Buist embankment — 7·4 — 4·6 — 16·1 Dunbar

After the first 2 km, follow signs for the John Muir Way (JMW) bike route southward from the A198 to just beyond Whitekirk; then head west to pick up signage for the John Muir Way walking route.

- From the ruins of St Andrew's Kirk, head east: depending on the state of the tide you may prefer to walk on the sands of the east beach or the pavement of Melbourne Road (later, Tantallon Terrace).

- After 1 km, pass the clubhouse of the Glen Golf Club and continue for a further 300 m along Tantallon Terrace to reach a car park (mile 0·9).

Porch of St Andrew's Kirk

- Cross the road to take the steep concrete steps up the slope ahead, leading to a path across the golf club's 18th hole. Continue inland on this path among houses, and follow a tarmac road named Lime Grove.

- After about 150 m the road meets the A198. Turn left along the main road, go past Tantallon Park caravans and a further 280 m after its entrance, at a fingerpost turn right on a minor road (Rhodes Holdings).

Blackdykes Farm buildings

- Follow this road south, as it makes a couple of doglegs past the pantiled buildings of Blackdykes Farm, resuming its southerly trend just after the farm. There are fine hedgerows, old stone walls and behind you views of North Berwick Law.
- Within 600 m, reach a T-junction where you go straight ahead on the No Through Road, signed for Gleghornie.
- That road descends and after 300 m turns left. Just 30 m later at mile 3·3, turn off right to continue south on a secluded narrow path known as Becky's Strip (signed JMW bike).
- Follow Becky's Strip for a total of 1·1 km, mostly enclosed between field edge and hedgerow, but with a central section across open field. About 250 m after you pass the entrance to Whitekirk Hill with its small pond you reach a large yard and pick up a tarmac access road.

Pond on Whitekirk Hill

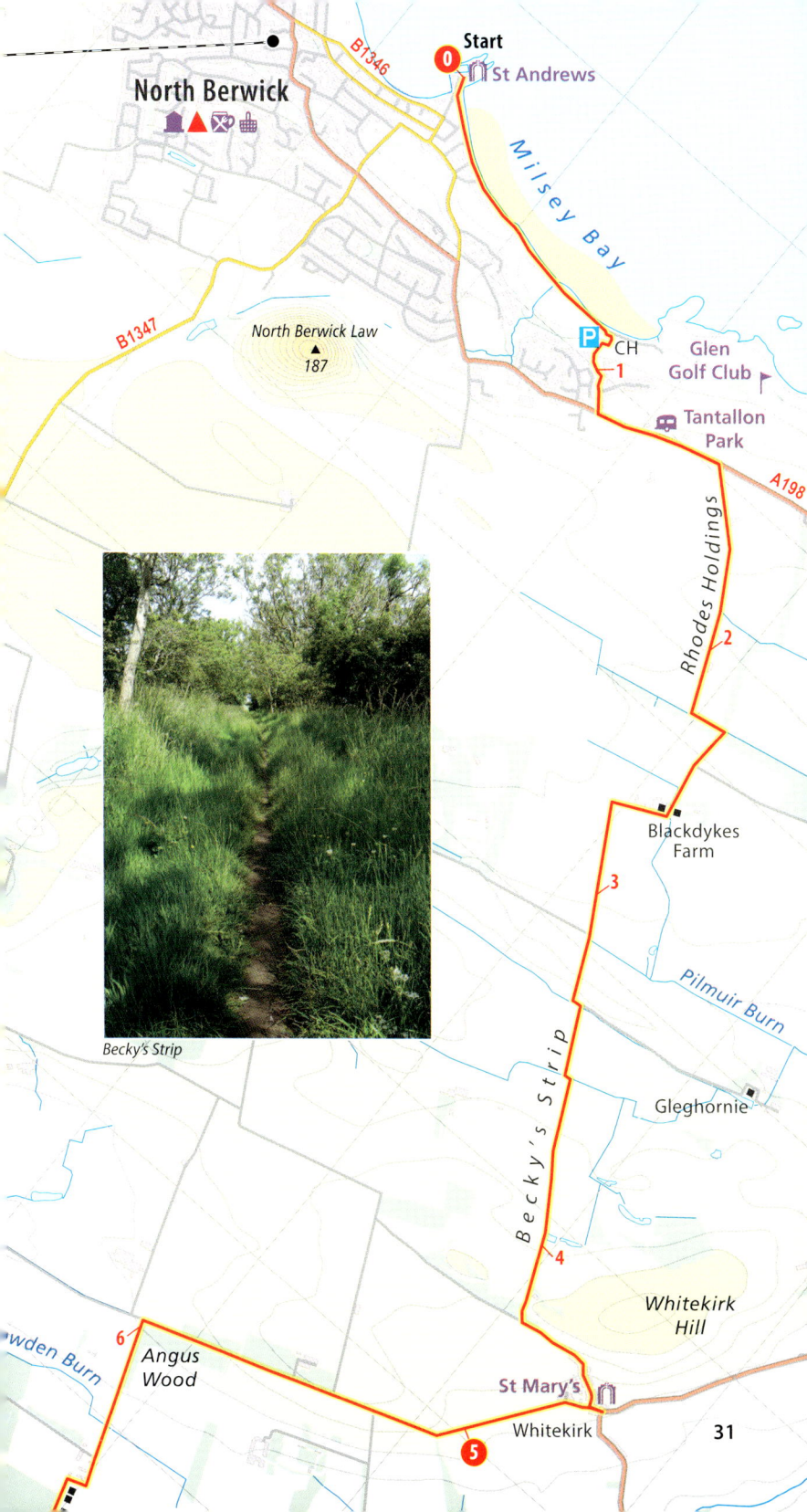

- This descends steeply to meet the public road. Turn left for Whitekirk and after 530 m reach a road junction: turn left for 50 m for St Mary's Parish Church, whose doors normally stand unlocked.

- From St Mary's, retrace your steps to the junction and keep straight on along the West Road: there is no verge, so walk on the right to face oncoming traffic. There is hedgerow to the right, with some open views to the left.

- After 1 km ignore the left-turn fingerpost signed East Linton/Binning Wood with JMW bike marker: instead keep ahead for a further 1·1 km. From here on you will instead follow the JMW walking route all the way into Dunbar.

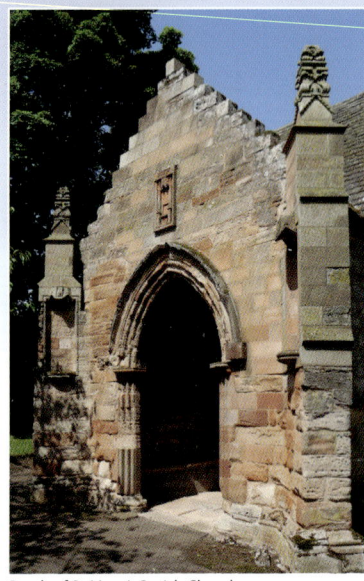
Porch of St Mary's Parish Church

- After the road descends gently past Angus Wood on your left, look for the old-style JMW sign 'John Muir Way, East Linton 2½ miles'.

- It takes you through a gate onto a cinder path running parallel to the access road to Kamehill Farm. The path soon joins the farm road. On approach to the farm buildings, take another path on the left so as to skirt the east side of the farm.

- Beyond the farm, cross two streams by timber bridges. Immediately after the second, the path turns right and continues through fields for 1·7 km. It climbs to a comms mast on Drylaw Hill (with a distant view of North Berwick Law behind you) before dropping to the B1377.

North from Drylaw Hill

Prestonkirk Parish Church

- As you approach the road, go left briefly on a channelled path (signed JMW), descend its steps and cross the road to reach the safety of the verge on the right.
- Walk down the road into East Linton and after 750 m turn left (north-east) onto Preston Road (signed Smeaton and JMW). After 350 m, the entrance to Prestonkirk Parish Church is on your left. This is a good place to split your journey if you have transport arrangements to suit.
- After the church, resume north-easterly on Preston Road. Within 100 m, opposite the entrance to Smeaton Nursery (with tearoom), turn right onto the JMW-signed access path for Preston Mill ('Dunbar 6¾').
- There is a panel about St Baldred's Well in the wall on your left. The path runs briefly beside the River Tyne before crossing the mill lade by a low timber footbridge.
- A further 70 m will take you to a taller footbridge over the River Tyne, but first make a 70-metre detour to look around the glorious landmark of Preston Mill.
- After the Mill, return to the footbridge to cross the Tyne and immediately turn left to follow the field-edge path, guided by JMW waymarkers. At first the river is on your left, but after skirting two sides of a field you recross the river and immediately turn right to follow the next field-edge path.

Preston Mill

33

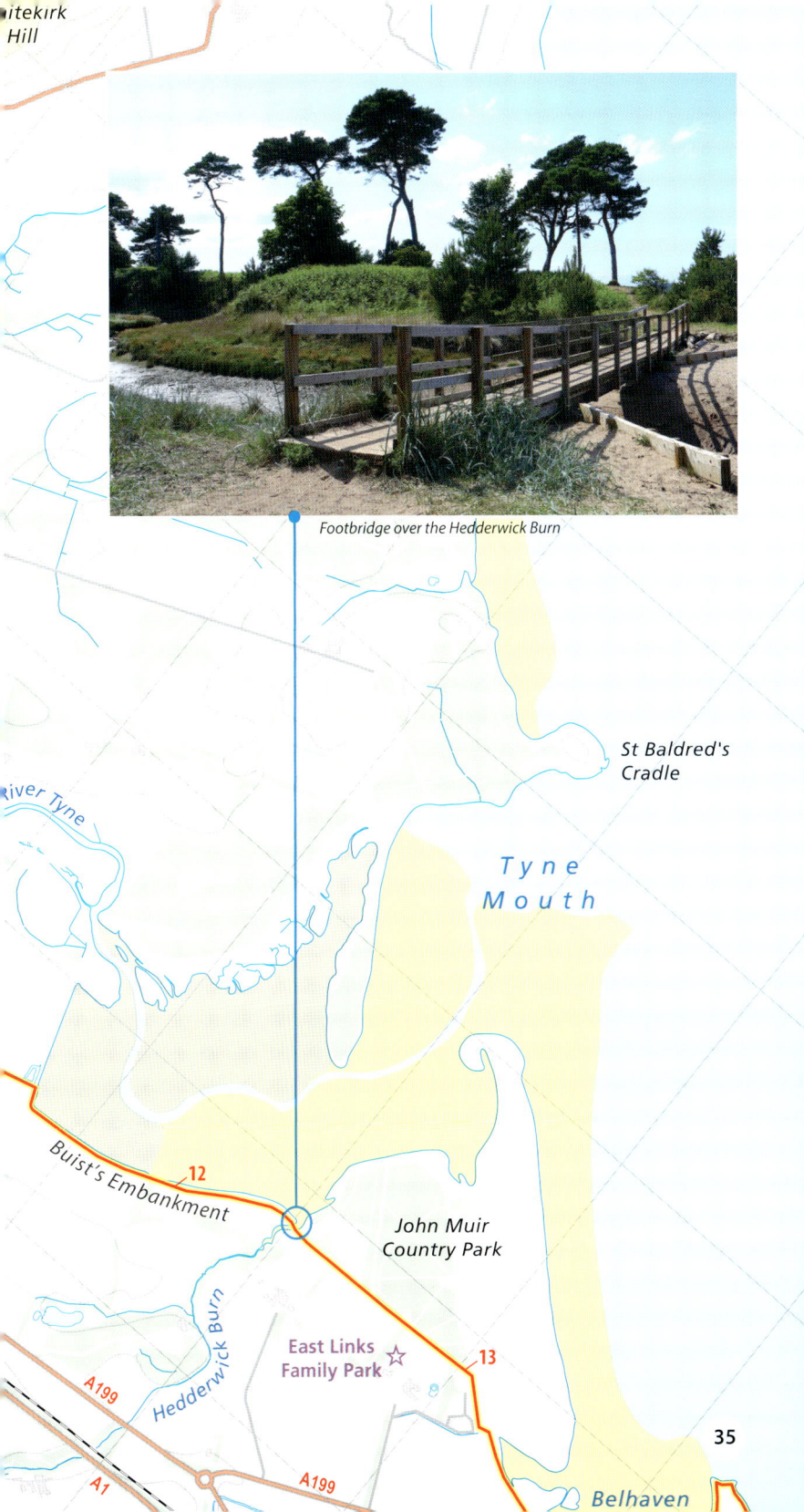
Footbridge over the Hedderwick Burn

St Baldred's Cradle

Tyne Mouth

Buist's Embankment

John Muir Country Park

East Links Family Park

Hedderwick Burn

Belhaven

35

- After a further 1 km with the river on your right, bear right towards the river with its red Dangerous Ford notice and cross by the footbridge to its left (mile 9·7).
- On its far side, follow the green Public Path Dunbar 5½/JMW sign to turn sharp left. Continue beside the River Tyne for a further 800 m to Tyninghame Bridge where you pass beneath the A198 road.

- Immediately after the bridge turn right along a field path beside the busy road. After 440 m turn left (east) along Ware Road. After 1·4 km this reaches Buist's Embankment, from the top of which you abruptly view the Tyne estuary, a mixture of mudflats, saltmarsh and water, depending on the state of the tide.
- A right-left dogleg takes you east on a narrow path just above Hedderwick Sands for 1·3 km. Take care near the low cliff-edge: coastal erosion creates danger in places.
- Cross the footbridge over the Hedderwick Burn to enter the John Muir Country Park. Continue east, either on the path at the right of the woodland or, if you prefer the lovely old Scots pines, on the parallel path through woodland. Pass the East Links Family Park on your right.

Minor landslip, Hedderwick Sands

- After 1 km beyond the footbridge, the path leaves the trees, bending right to pass above the saltmarsh and sands of Belhaven Bay. (Please don't cut across this fragile beach area, even if the tide is out.) Follow JMW signs on the inland route: within 800 m it detours briefly to a footbridge across the Biel Water.

Scots pines, John Muir Country Park

- The route resumes easterly along the edge of the Belhaven Bay Caravan Park. After 500 m, turn left along Shore Road at a fingerpost. Pass its car park, and when you reach a point above the beach footbridge, follow the road as it turns right and ends in another car park.
- Keep ahead on a narrow path, cobbled at first, to skirt around Winterfield Golf Club on its seaward side for the next 1·5 km. Follow the red poles closely, taking care to avoid disturbing play and staying vigilant for errant golf balls.

- The views on your left range from North Berwick Law to the Bass Rock and the North Sea, with the Isle of May about 14 miles/23 km to the north, its lighthouse prominent on a clear day.
- Follow the red poles to pass beneath the clubhouse and, at the last pole, climb the wooden staircase to the clifftop to pass beside Winterfield Park. The entire esplanade was gifted to the town in 1893 by Mrs Jane Baird: see the wall plaque near the end of the tarmac.

- Continue ahead on the path along the Clifftop Trail: for a useful booklet see page 71. Below and to your left, the rocky beach area is known as 'the Bathe' after the wild swimming pool in which hardy Victorians swam. At low tide the outline of this semi-natural hollow is obvious.
- To your right is Dunbar's War Memorial, set on a base of 'Dunbar marble' (fossil-rich limestone). First erected on a rocky outcrop in 1921, it was moved inland in the 1980s to save it from erosion.
- Fine coastal views include the Forth and across to Fife, as you approach the centre of Dunbar. After a further 300 m, leave the Clifftop Trail to cross Bayswell Park diagonally, aiming for a flight of steps that you climb to emerge between sandstone obelisks.

War Memorial, Dunbar

Rock pools and 'the Bathe'

- Turn left along Bayswell Road, which soon bends right and leads into Dunbar High Street. Pass (or visit) the John Muir Birthplace at number 126: see panel.
- Keep south on the High Street, perhaps crossing over to the uplifting statue of John Muir that stands outside the Town House (museum and gallery).
- Within 200 m of the statue, bear left at the fork. (Bearing right instead would bring you within 300 m to Station Road and Dunbar's mainline railway.) After 200 m you reach Dunbar Parish Church on the right.

Statue of John Muir, Dunbar

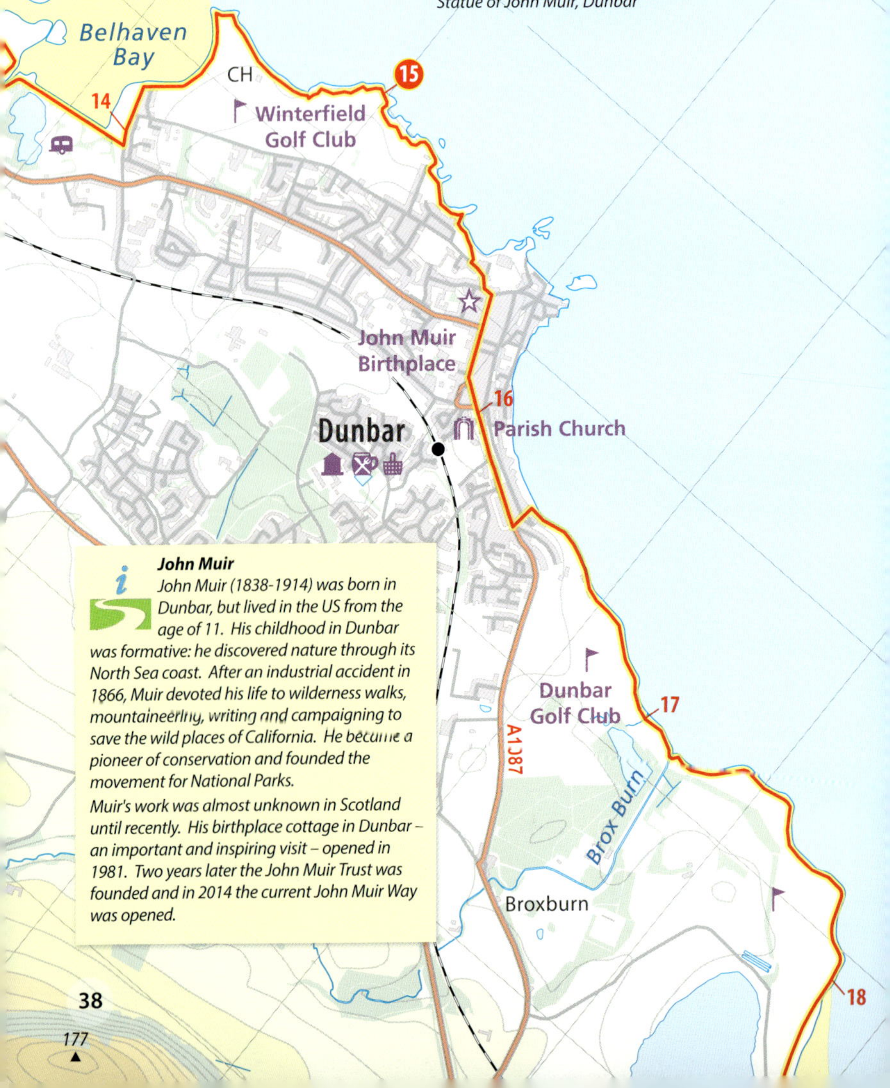

John Muir

John Muir (1838-1914) was born in Dunbar, but lived in the US from the age of 11. His childhood in Dunbar was formative: he discovered nature through its North Sea coast. After an industrial accident in 1866, Muir devoted his life to wilderness walks, mountaineering, writing and campaigning to save the wild places of California. He became a pioneer of conservation and founded the movement for National Parks.

Muir's work was almost unknown in Scotland until recently. His birthplace cottage in Dunbar – an important and inspiring visit – opened in 1981. Two years later the John Muir Trust was founded and in 2014 the current John Muir Way was opened.

3·2 Dunbar to Cockburnspath

Distance	10·2 miles 16·4 km
Terrain	mixture of tarmac, grassy paths and farm tracks
Grade	mainly level or gently undulating
Food and drink	Dunbar (wide range), Cockburnspath (shop)
Side-trip	Dunglass Collegiate Church
Summary	coastal traverse of golf courses and beaches with woodland interludes; ends at Cockburnspath's historic Square and parish church

16·1 — Dunbar — 3·3 / 5·3 — Barns Ness — 2·3 / 3·7 — Torness — 2·7 / 4·3 — Bilsdean Burn — 1·9 / 3·1 — Cockburnspath — 26·3

At first, follow signs for the John Muir Link (JML); afterwards follow old signs that show the former route of the Southern Upland Way (SUW) into Cockburnspath.

- From Dunbar Parish Church, continue south-east on Queen's Road for nearly 400 m and turn sharp left (signed JML) onto Golf House Road (mile 16·4), and descend to the shore.

- Turn right onto the concrete promenade that runs on the beach side of the stone wall. It soon narrows to a gap stile, after which you reach safety notices for Dunbar Golf Club (established in 1856). Please observe their requests: stay alert for golf balls, and defer to golf play, for the next 2·7 km.

Gap stile on the promenade

- Follow closely the red stakes that mark the path around the golf course, after 800 m crossing the Brox Burn by a bridge. Two manmade landmarks start to appear ahead: to the left the slender tower of Barns Ness Lighthouse and to the right, the chunky cuboids of Torness nuclear power station.

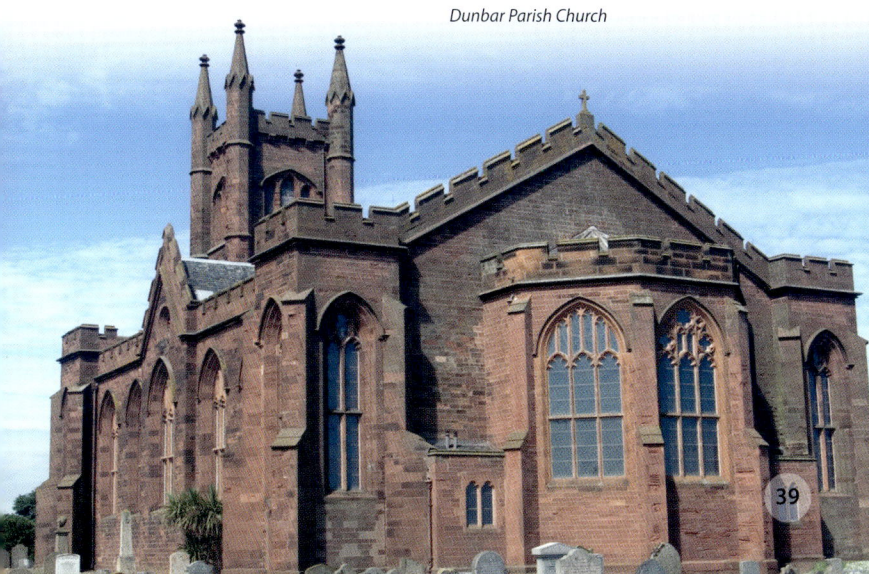

Dunbar Parish Church

- Soon after a ruined stone building on the right, you reach the end of the golf course and emerge on a sandy path above the beach.
- The Way veers away from the shore, and you take a well-defined path parallel to the road just short of the tarmac. (If you overshoot, it doesn't matter: just use the road.)
- At another JM Link fingerpost, reach a tarmac road and turn left towards White Sands Bay where there is a Catcraig Geology Trail with nine kinds of limestone on the foreshore.
- Bear left to approach the Barns Ness Lighthouse, built in 1901 by David Alan Stevenson, cousin of author Robert Louis Stevenson and a prolific lighthouse builder.
- After the lighthouse, continue for nearly 2 km on the path between a fence and the back of the dunes, to a footbridge across the so-called 'Dry Burn' – a flowing river at mile 20·5.
- Beyond the footbridge, go past Skateraw Farm's field on your right, and after 300 m turn right (unsigned) at its corner, where there are stiles and a bench. Cut across Chapel Point and go around Skateraw Bay towards Torness.
- Keep ahead on the tarmac road towards Skateraw car park with toilets and information board (mile 21·4). You approach the nuclear power station by climbing gently on a fenced path. There's a well preserved lime kiln on the left, with its own info board.

Eastern end of the golf course

Barns Ness Lighthouse

Across Skateraw Bay to Torness

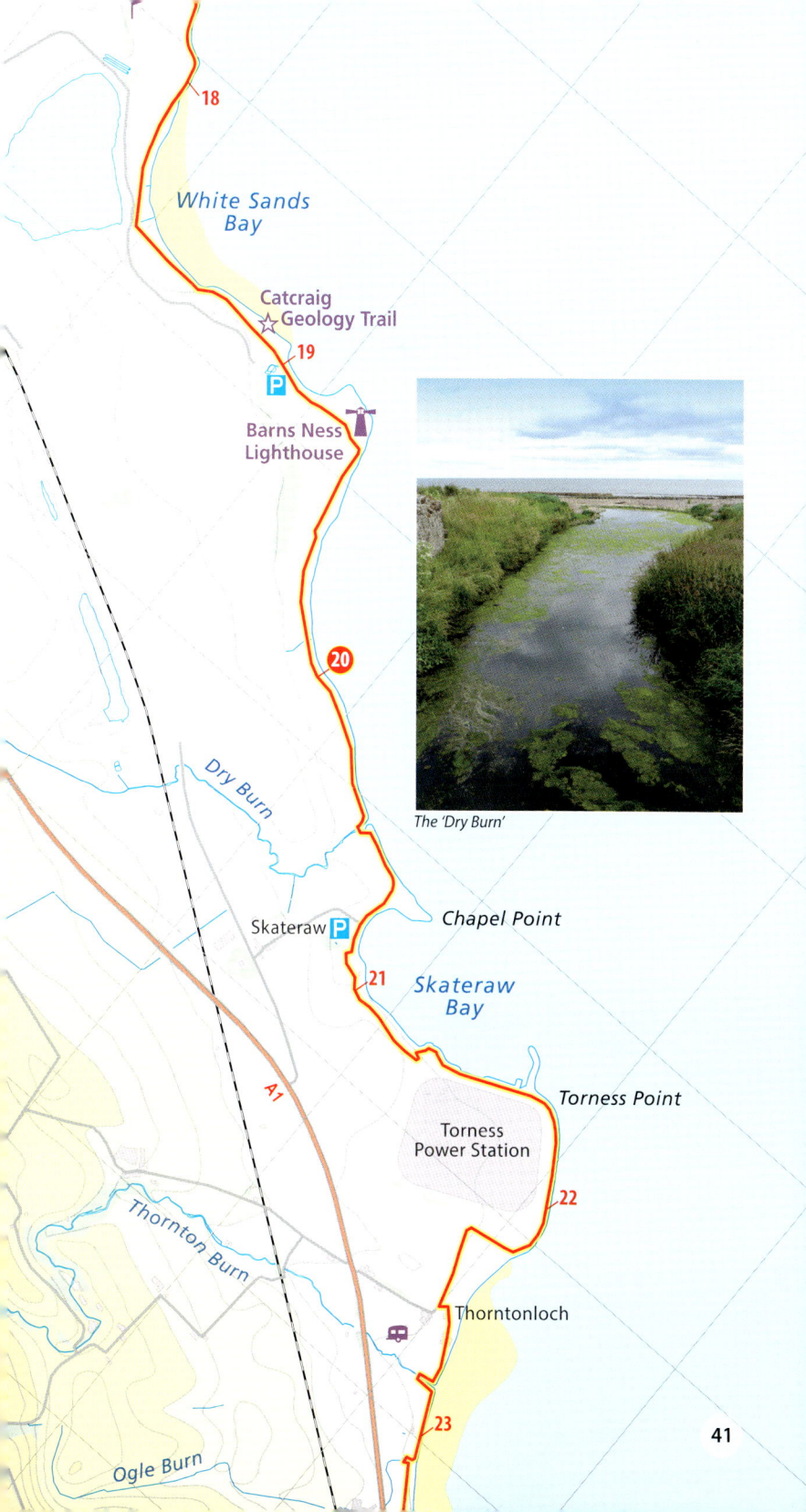

The 'Dry Burn'

41

- After 400 m the path zigzags downhill on broad steps to shore level. Head across to the manmade walkway that follows the perimeter of the licensed nuclear site on its shore side. There are high-level sections (advised in stormy weather and around high tide) and low-level sections (preferable in calm conditions).

- Heading inland you approach the employee car park but turn left just beforehand, now heading south parallel to the coast. Within 400 m make a left-right dogleg to pass through Thorntonloch Caravan Park where the route is also signed. (If the tide is out, you could instead head down to the beach and pass below the caravan park.)

- Cross Thornton Burn by a footbridge that lies slightly inland, then continue along the beach on a mixture of sand and shingle. About 300 m later, detour inland briefly to cross the Ogle Burn by another footbridge and climb steeply to the final clifftop section.

- With sandstone cliffs on your left, arable fields to the right and St Abb's Head distant ahead, enjoy scenic coastal walking for about 2 km. At mile 24·4 the route heads inland and takes an unexpected sylvan interlude in The Linn, a densely wooded gorge created by the Bilsdean Burn.

- Descend past falls and rapids and emerge on a pebbly beach with the remains of Castle Dykes Iron Age fort above.

- Follow the beach for 500 m, then look on the right for a John Muir Link fingerpost turning you inland up a narrow steep path (mile 24·8). (If you reach Dunglass Burn, you have overshot: backtrack to find the fingerpost.)

Through the Linn

- Follow the path uphill, bearing left at first and inland, with the Dunglass Burn below you to the left. Go up through trees and through a kissing-gate, to reach another John Muir Link fingerpost.
- The path now passes under three bridges (two road bridges and a railway viaduct) to reach a tarmac road. The John Muir Link ends nearby on the A1, but the F2F follows old timber fingerposts for the Southern Upland Way (long since rerouted).
- To continue the Way, follow the next bullet, but first we recommend a short detour to Dunglass Collegiate Church: see panel on page 44. Cross the road, pass through the gate ahead and walk up its access drive for 400 m. Retrace your steps afterwards, turn right for 90 m across the road bridge and skip the next bullet.
- Otherwise, turn left to follow the road for just 90 m to the far side of the road bridge over Dunglass Burn.
- At the old SUW fingerpost, turn right offroad on a rough track that climbs through the woods of Dunglass Dean for 550 m.
- Look out for the next old SUW fingerpost at mile 25·5, where you turn left to exit the wood across open hillside. Within 120 m climb to go through an unsigned low timber gate on your right, into Eildbalks Wood.
- Follow the path along the northern edge of the wood for 600 m, high above the fields with fine views in places. Keep ahead as it leads into Callander Place, Cockburnspath.
- Continue for 120 m to cross The Square and its historic cross. Follow a lane off its south side to reach Cockburnspath Parish Church.

Railway viaduct

Through Dunglass Dean

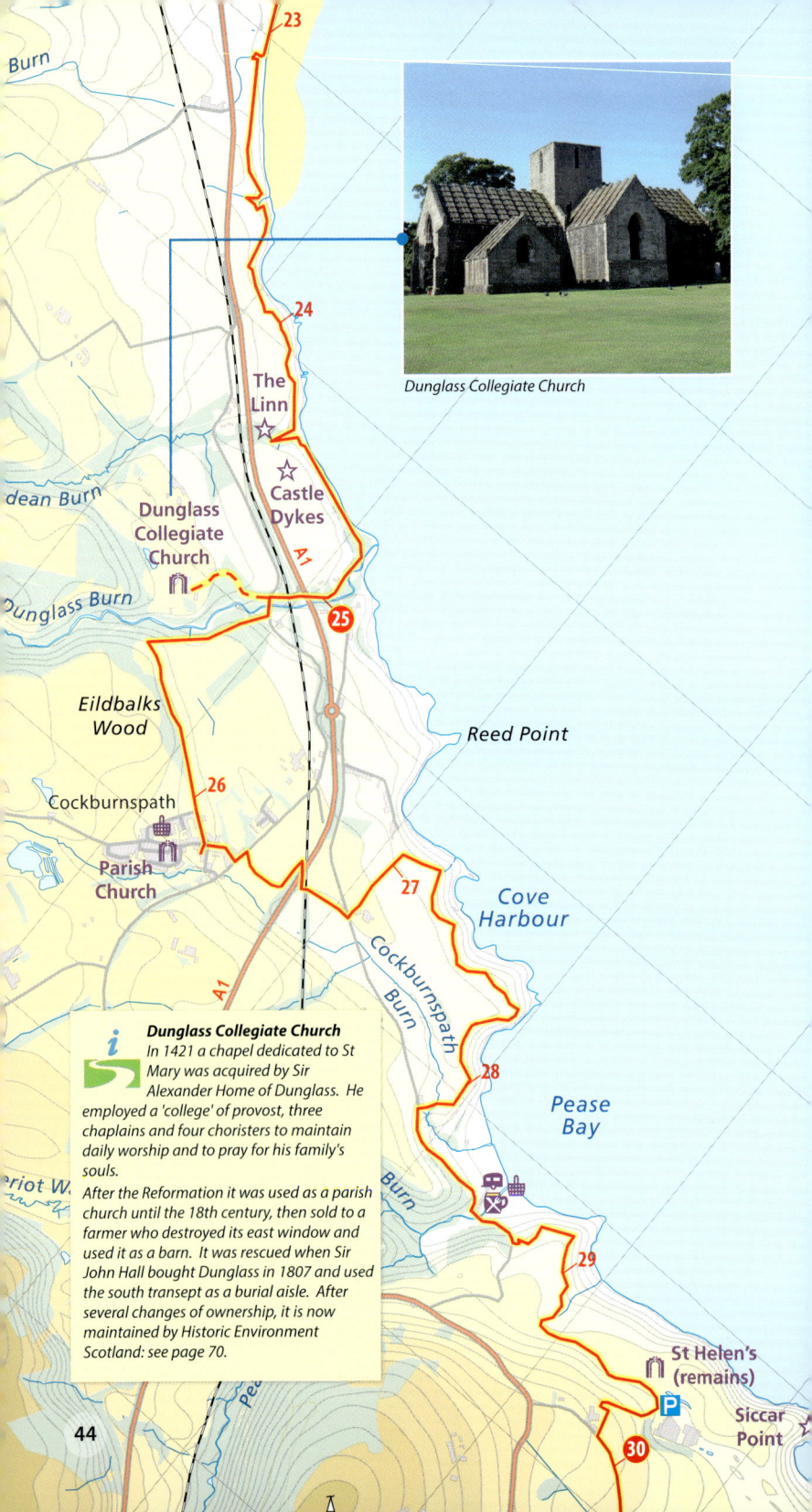

Dunglass Collegiate Church

Dunglass Collegiate Church
In 1421 a chapel dedicated to St Mary was acquired by Sir Alexander Home of Dunglass. He employed a 'college' of provost, three chaplains and four choristers to maintain daily worship and to pray for his family's souls.

After the Reformation it was used as a parish church until the 18th century, then sold to a farmer who destroyed its east window and used it as a barn. It was rescued when Sir John Hall bought Dunglass in 1807 and used the south transept as a burial aisle. After several changes of ownership, it is now maintained by Historic Environment Scotland: see page 70.

Cockburnspath

East from the Way into Cockburnspath

In 1503 King James IV of Scotland erected the Mercat Cross in Cockburnspath's Square. It celebrates his marriage to Margaret Tudor, sister of Henry VIII of England, to whom he gifted lands around Cockburnspath in her dowry. Their union was known as the marriage of the Thistle and the Rose, national emblems that are carved on this cross. It led to the Union of Scottish and English crowns a century later, when their great-grandson James VI of Scotland inherited also the English throne.

Cockburnspath Parish Church is one of Scotland's few pre-Reformation churches. It may date back to the 14th or early 15th century, but was extensively rebuilt in the 19th century. Its distinctive round tower probably dates from the late 16th century, and is built into the full height of the much earlier west gable.

Mercat cross, the Square

Less known is the village's connection with the Glasgow Boys, a collective of about 20 artists whose work challenged the artistic conventions of their time. Many of them relocated to Cockburnspath in 1883, where the light suited their fresh, innovative style and authentic rural life provided natural subjects. James Guthrie (1859-1930) was one of the leading members and he lived in the village from 1883-85, where he painted some of his most important works.

Cockburnspath Parish Church

3.3 Cockburnspath to St Abbs

| | | | 44 | 47 | 49 | 53 |

Distance	13·6 miles 21·9 km
Terrain	mainly grassy paths with farm tracks and some minor road; many gates and stiles will slow you down
Grade	undulating slopes, steep in places
Food and drink	Cockburnspath (shop), St Abbs
Side-trip	Fast Castle (from Dowlaw Farm)
Summary	mostly coastal with some inland detours, leading to the grandeur of St Abb's headland, lighthouse and nature reserve

26·3 — 2·2 — 2·6 — 2·7 — 2·5 — 3·6 — 39·9
Cockburnspath 3·5 Pease Bay 4·2 Redheugh Farm 4·3 Dowlaw Farm 4·0 Moor Burn 5·8 St Abbs

Follow signs for the Southern Upland Way (SUW) for the first 2·4 miles (3·8 km), then follow the blue circular logo for the Berwickshire Coastal Path (BCP).

- After Cockburnspath Parish Church, return to The Square and turn right along Hoprig Road. After 170 m reach the junction with Edinburgh Road, with a war memorial across the road and a Southern Upland Way information board on the right.

- Make a left-right dogleg, following the Edinburgh Road for just 70 m before turning right on the informal farm road (sign may be obscured).

- Follow this round to the left and after 400 m pass under the A1. Now make a right-left dogleg to pass under the railway line following the thistle-in-hexagon logo ❶.

- Within 230 m, reach a junction and cross the road in a left-right dogleg to a grassy lane with the first BCP sign ❷. Descend it for 600 m to the coast. Views to the north include Torness and the Bass Rock.

- Turn right to follow the coastline as signed for 1·6 km, at first on a clifftop path with a view of Cove Harbour, then on a mixture of field-edge and clifftop paths.

North-west over Pease Bay

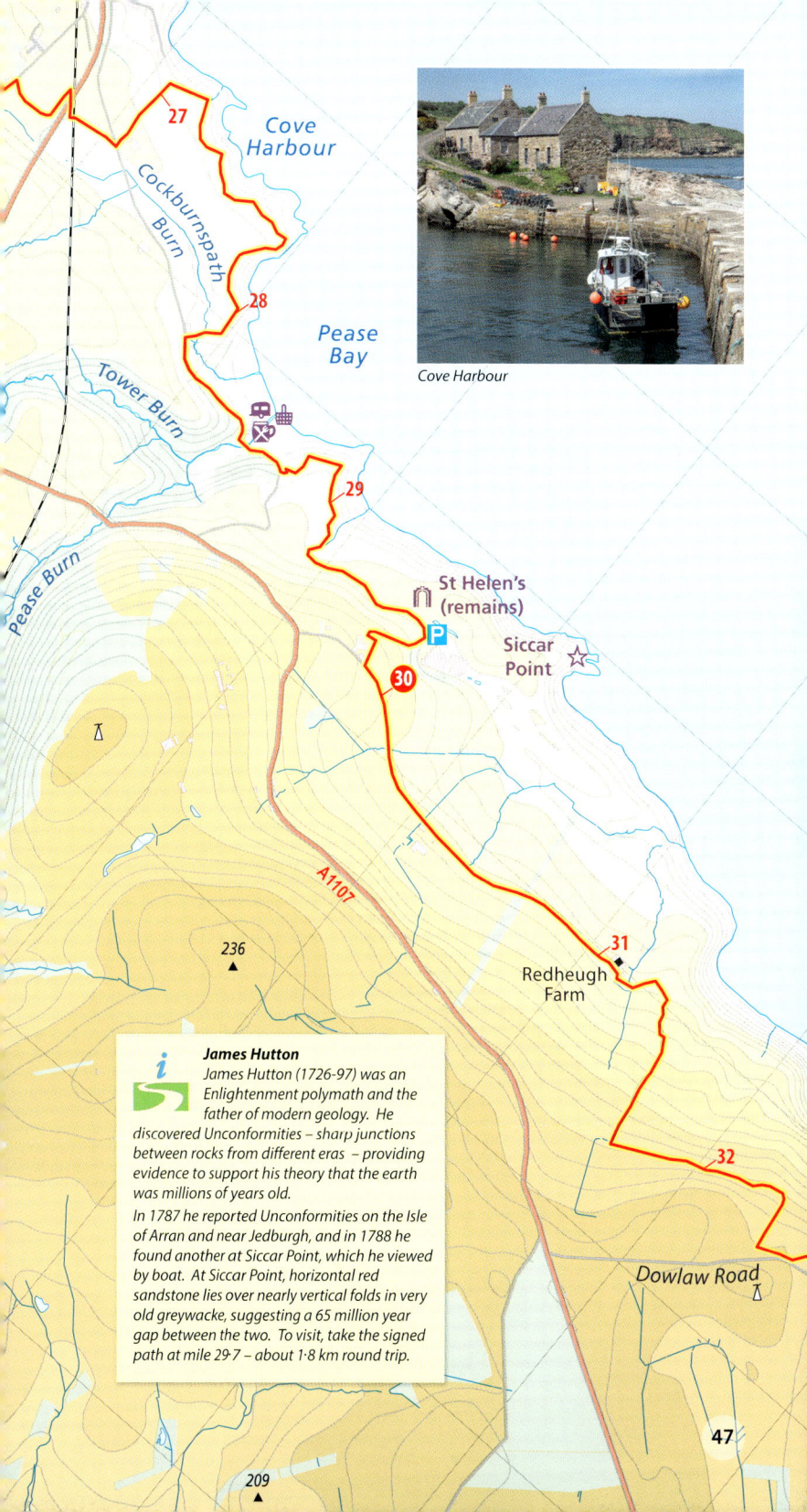

Cove Harbour

James Hutton

James Hutton (1726-97) was an Enlightenment polymath and the father of modern geology. He discovered Unconformities – sharp junctions between rocks from different eras – providing evidence to support his theory that the earth was millions of years old.

In 1787 he reported Unconformities on the Isle of Arran and near Jedburgh, and in 1788 he found another at Siccar Point, which he viewed by boat. At Siccar Point, horizontal red sandstone lies over nearly vertical folds in very old greywacke, suggesting a 65 million year gap between the two. To visit, take the signed path at mile 29·7 – about 1·8 km round trip.

- After a flight of steps down to a burn, climb to a kissing-gate and reach a tarmac road.
- Turn left down the road towards Pease Bay Leisure Park. At the bottom of the hill ignore the Southern Upland Way that turns off inland: keep ahead on the road.
- Cross a forded stream by a footbridge, and continue uphill. After 250 m on the road, take the path on the left that soon climbs steeply by steps to regain the clifftop.

- Follow BCP signs as the path takes you around the clifftop, after about 800 m turning inland to reach a tarmac road.
- Turn left along the road to reach the entrance to the Siccar Point walk, with info board and parking area: see the panel on page 47.
- Just afterwards, at a fingerpost (mile 29·7) bear right off the road, heading up a rough track that climbs steeply. Follow the track uphill, bearing left as signed on a vague path leading to a gate.
- Turn right towards the buildings and follow a field-edge path to reach another tarmac road at mile 29·9.
- Turn left along the narrow road with fine hawthorn hedgerows for 1·9 km to pass through Redheugh Farm.
- After the farmyard, go through a gate and pass a duck pond on your right. Follow the farm road for a further 250 m where you turn right off it, just before a water course.
- Keep the water course on your left as you climb. Do not cross until after a kissing-gate and a further climb to a clump of oak trees. Here a fingerpost sends you across to its far side, still climbing on a field-edge path.
- After about 800 m of climbing, turn left at mile 31·6 along field-edge paths punctuated by kissing-gates for a further 800 m. Turn right at mile 32·2 towards a comms mast (on the far side of Dowlaw Road) but before the road, turn left on a field-edge path for nearly 200 m to a waymarker.

North-west over the coast, Torness distant

- At this point the BCP points straight ahead, but here, or at the next waymarker (mile 32·6), you could instead bear right to pick up the narrow, quiet road for quicker walking. As of late 2020 the path was very overgrown, barely visible in places and devoid of waymarkers. In poor visibility the road may be a better choice. The height of this section (215 m) makes it prone to sea fog.

Trod path through the heather

- If conditions are good and you stay on the offroad path, expect slow progress over broken ground on an ill-defined trod path with dense vegetation. Enjoy fine coastal views, especially behind you.
- Wherever you return to the road, turn left to head for Dowlaw Farm, which is about 3 km away from the comms mast. In front of the farm, ignore the sign pointing left (unless you want to detour to the ruins of Fast Castle).

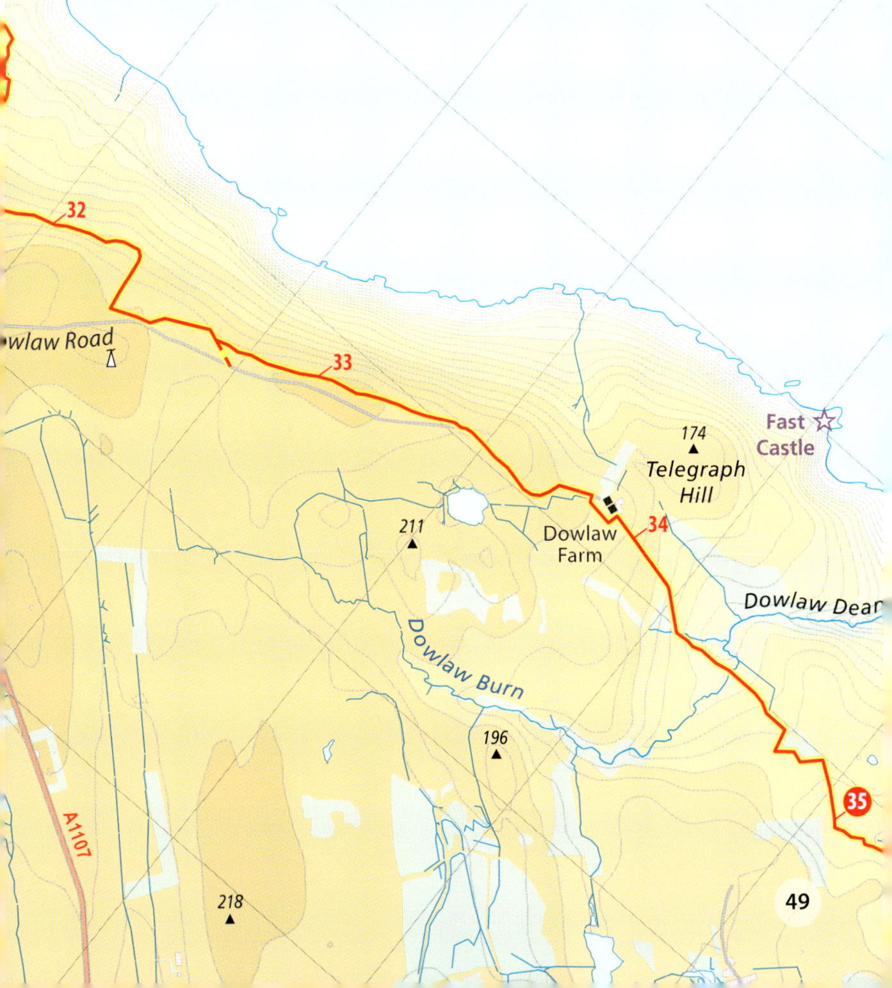

- The fingerpost promises St Abbs in 6¼ miles and sends you through a small gate on the right. The path leads through a small wood, bypassing the farm buildings.
- Emerging from the wood, follow signs taking you generally eastward for about 2 km of field-edge paths. Within 900 m you descend to cross Dowlaw Burn by a concrete footbridge, with a fine old stone bridge up to your left.
- Over the next 1·3 km there's a slight climb and a number of bends around field corners before you descend to the coastal clifftop at Rough Heugh.
- The route now stays close to the clifftop for the next 3 miles/5 km with frequent BCP signs to guide you through gates and over stiles. There are grand views over the coast behind you, to your left, and soon also ahead, where St Abb's headland comes into view.
- After about 1·8 km, you approach a major obstacle: the deep ravine of Westerside Dean (mile 36·2). Drop down to the corner of a field and follow the fingerpost ★ that sends you through a gate. The path descends unexpectedly towards a headland, dropping steeply in places.

Stone bridge over Dowlaw Burn

Footbridge over the Moor Burn

Fingerpost at field corner

- Your goal soon becomes obvious: a timber footbridge provides the only way to cross the Moor Burn. On its far side, climb the trod path and turn right beside a stone wall for about 100 m.
- Then turn left to start the long, steep climb back to clifftop level. You gain 90 m of altitude over 250 m of rough ground.
- After the main climb, make a right-left dogleg as signed and, still climbing, pick your way among or around some dense gorse, soon gaining views of Coldingham Loch ahead.

Coastal cliffs

- Descend to the stile and footbridge over its outflow burn, climbing again afterwards. Head towards the lower of a second pair of Admiralty distance poles in a field. It's worth looking behind you from time to time for views over the cliffs.
- Skirt the field corner and continue ahead, with ever improving views of the headland. The trail now makes a long descent all the way to 25 m above sea level, crossing some wall stiles on the way down.

Ladder stile on the descent

- At a fingerpost in the bottom corner you meet the tarmac access road in St Abb's Head National Nature Reserve.
- Turn left along the road that snakes its way up towards the headland, with grand views over the historic tiny harbour of Pettico Wick to your left: see photo on pp4-5. Soon you see over Mire Loch, the manmade loch that appears on our front cover.

Road snaking up to St Abb's Head

- On a clear day, the views behind you (north-west) include Torness and, to its right Barns Ness lighthouse with the Fife peninsula beyond. The photo below shows Fife's summit over 40 miles away – West Lomond (522 m) – aligned with Barns Ness.

View north-west to Fife

- After 650 m the road ends at the famous St Abb's Lighthouse, unusual in that it's reached by a downward flight of steps: see page 22. It has protected that headland since 1862 and its light was automated in 1993.
- Take the steep path up behind the lighthouse to pick up a path signed as the Lighthouse Loop. It passes some dramatic coves before heading slightly inland to climb the shoulder of Kirk Hill: this is where St Ebba founded her church: see page 16.
- Descend to the coast at Horsecastle Bay. Enjoy another 1 km of superb coastal scenery before you reach a picnic area where the path turns right inland (now suited to 'All Abilities'). Reach the B6438 public road within 300 m.
- Cross over and turn left (at first on a roadside footpath) to descend into St Abbs past the gateway to Northfield House: see page 16. It belonged to Andrew Usher (1826-1898) who generously restored the harbour in 1890. Soon you reach the Visitor Centre on the left where you can learn more about the village and Usher: see the panel opposite.

North-east to the first headland

Coastal scenery near mile 39

St Abb's Lighthouse with foghorn beneath

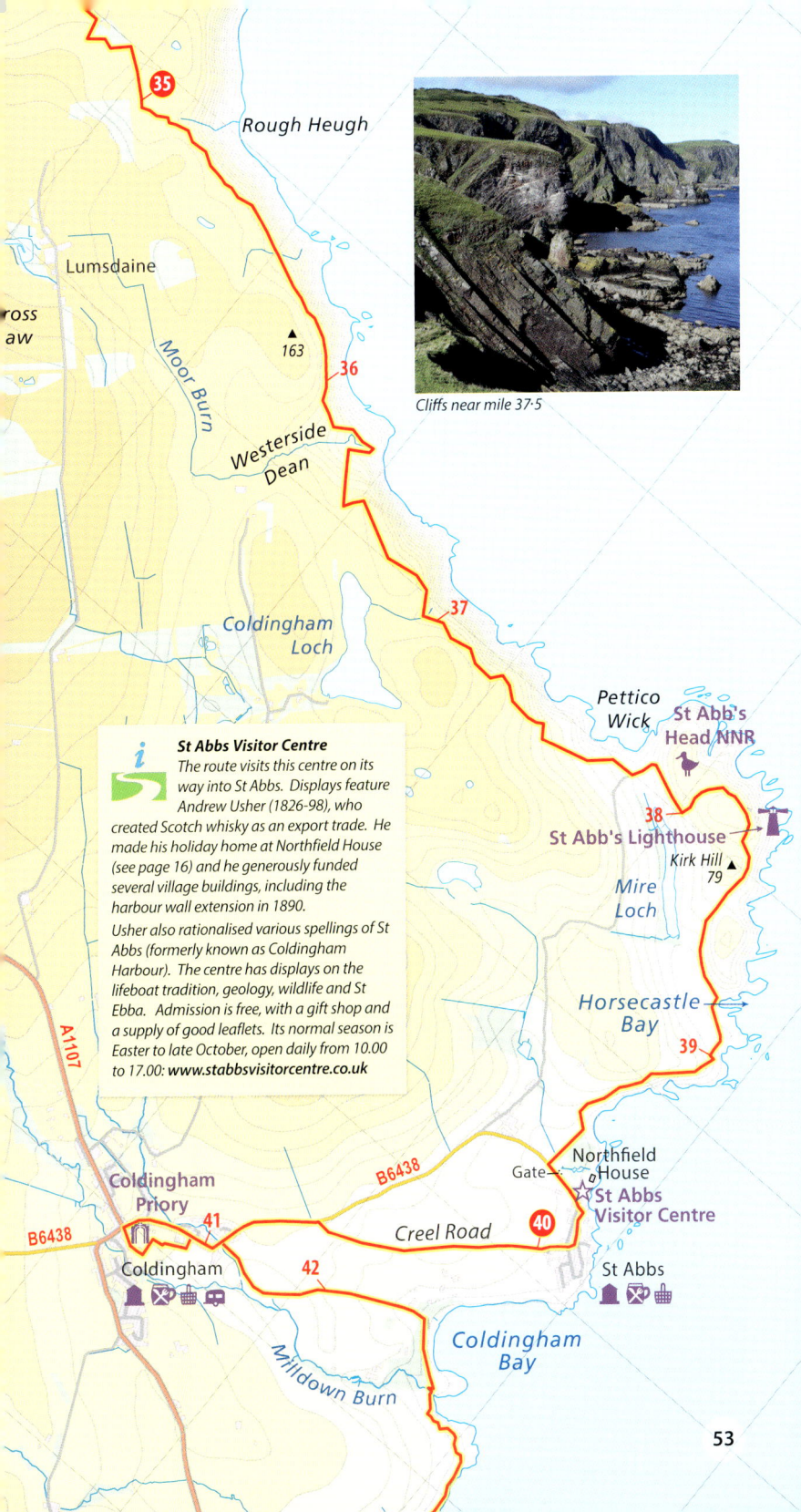

Cliffs near mile 37·5

St Abbs Visitor Centre

The route visits this centre on its way into St Abbs. Displays feature Andrew Usher (1826-98), who created Scotch whisky as an export trade. He made his holiday home at Northfield House (see page 16) and he generously funded several village buildings, including the harbour wall extension in 1890.

Usher also rationalised various spellings of St Abbs (formerly known as Coldingham Harbour). The centre has displays on the lifeboat tradition, geology, wildlife and St Ebba. Admission is free, with a gift shop and a supply of good leaflets. Its normal season is Easter to late October, open daily from 10.00 to 17.00: www.stabbsvisitorcentre.co.uk

3.4 St Abbs to Berwick upon Tweed

Distance	16·1 miles 25·9 km
Terrain	mainly grassy paths with farm tracks and some tarmac
Grade	undulating slopes, steep in places
Food and drink	St Abbs, Coldingham, Eyemouth, Burnmouth (First & Last), Berwick (wide range)
Summary	after Coldingham, the route stays coastal along beaches, promenade and clifftop golf courses, crossing the border into England

39·9 — 1·5 — 4·3 — 3·3 — 3·1 — 3·9 — 56·0
St Abbs 2·4 Coldingham Priory 6·9 Eye Water 5·3 Burnmouth 5·0 The Border 6·3 Berwick

Mostly you follow the blue circular logo for the Berwickshire Coastal Path (BCP), except briefly at the start (when the F2F visits Coldingham) and end (when the F2F follows Berwick's ramparts) and there are no signs.

 This section contains several places with exposed cliff edges. Care is needed, especially in poor visibility, high winds or if your sense of balance is uncertain.

- Just beyond the Visitor Centre, the road divides: turn right along the higher option, overlooking the harbours. After 150 m turn right onto a road that soon becomes Creel Road (mile 39·9).

- Unless you are very pressed for time, ignore the BCP fingerpost just below this junction that points to Coldingham by the coastal route. This shortcut would rejoin the F2F at Coldingham Bay, see the foot of page 56 – at the price of missing the conservation village of Coldingham and its glorious Priory.

- Creel Road's tarmac ends after 150 m, but the Way continues ahead on the narrow path 'Creel Road'. Stay on this historic path, used by monks and fishermen, for 1 km to reach the B6438. At first it is channelled between fields, then becomes enclosed as it tunnels through the trees and shrubs.

The secluded Creel Road

Coldingham Priory

- Turn left along the B6438, after 500 m noticing the signs for the road that turns left down to Coldingham Sands. This will be your exit route after visiting Coldingham.
- Continue for a further 500 m into the centre of Coldingham to the point where the main road (High Street) is joined by School Road from the right. Coldingham Priory and its church are obvious on the left: follow the sign.
- Walk around Coldingham Priory, which has many info boards that explain its intriguing history: see page 16-17. When finished, leave by the path at the rear, passing through the cemetery and Priory Garden.
- Exit on a narrow walled path that soon becomes broader and bends left to become a road (Fisher's Brae). Within 50 m reach St Abbs Road where you turn right.
- After 160 m, just after the entrance to Scoutscroft Holiday Park, turn right down the road to Coldingham Sands mentioned at top of this page.
- This descends past the caravans within 1·1 km to reach Coldingham Bay. This is a popular spot for surfing, and in season the beach café to the right is normally open.

Coldingham Bay

Bay with beach and footbridge

- To continue the route, turn right along the top of the beach and follow BCP signs over the rise, down into a small bay with a pebbly beach.
- At its far end, take the wooden steps up the steep slope and follow the path to the next, larger bay where you drop down onto the beach.
- Just before the red sandstone outcrop at the end of the beach, take the path inland up a steepish valley, with timber steps and a footbridge over the burn.

Outcrop at the end of the beach

- At the top of the valley the path turns left and skirts around the edge of fields at clifftop level, beside a stone wall in places. Follow the long, level field-edge path until you reach Eyemouth Holiday Park (caravans).
- Turn left on the track that skirts around the coastal edge of the holiday park for about 1 km. After rounding the headland with Eyemouth Fort, the track ends by dropping down a slope by steps to reach Eyemouth Bay promenade.
- Continue along the promenade, known here as The Bantry, past a group of memorial bronze statues: see page 21.
- Around the corner beside the harbour, follow Marine Parade, then Harbour Road. Detour right up Manse Road for the museum: see panel.

> **Eyemouth Museum**
> After Berwick was lost to England in 1482, Eyemouth became Scotland's largest south-east port. Fishing was always at its heart, and this museum shows a reconstructed fisherman's family home. It also displays the splendid Eyemouth Tapestry, created in memory of the 1881 disaster: see page 21.
>
> Eyemouth Fort was built in 1547 by English troops after a short war, but was demolished in 1550. Rising tensions between Scotland, England and France led to a rebuild, and the museum's interactive 3-D display recreates the fort's history. The building also houses a gallery and visitor information. In 2020, it was open April to October 11.00 to 16.00 Mon to Sat, with a small admission charge:
> **www.eyemouthmuseum.co.uk**.

Eyemouth harbour

- Just after Quayside Chandlery, cross the harbour onto Middle Pier, then cross Red Bridge and turn left to pass in front of Gunsgreen House (or visit, see page 23). After 100 m, climb steps on your right and turn right, soon to pass Nisbet's Tower.

- Just afterwards, turn left up John's Road, and after 90 m turn left on the access drive of the football club. At its fence, make a left-right dogleg to reach a road within 100 m: turn right along its footpath.

- After 160 m beside the road, cross over and enter Eyemouth Golf Club on a sheltered path that reaches the coast within 250 m. Follow the coast and enjoy the spectacular scenery while remaining alert to golf balls and players. Behind you, St Abb's Lighthouse remains visible over a surprising distance.

- Mostly you are walking between the golf course boundary wall and cliff edge, signed 'Smugglers' Trail'. In places you are signed to the inside of the wall for safety from exposed or unstable cliff edges.

- After the golf course, begin a steady climb up to the dramatic cliffs at Blaikie Heugh, rising to 103 m above the sea.

Gunsgreen House Smugglers Museum

Sign to detour inside the wall

- The route still undulates over the next 2 km into Burnmouth, but on trend it descends. On the final approach it goes unexpectedly inland on a field-edge path, then drops down into the village.

- Descend past Burnmouth Primary School and make a left-right dogleg to follow the road that descends a 20% slope to the harbour, signed for Lower Burnmouth and Cowdrait. (However, if you want to reach the First & Last pub – about 400 m away – instead make a right-left dogleg on the road at this upper level.)

Steps descend towards Burnmouth

- After the descent you pass the outer and inner harbours of Lower Burnmouth (mile 49·3). Near the harbour wall there are several memorials to the 1881 fishing disaster including more bronze figures like those in St Abbs and Eyemouth.

- After the sign for Cowdrait about 300 m later, start looking for house numbers. Between houses 18 and 19 take a signed path on wooden steps up the steep slope between their back gardens (mile 49·6).

- After the steps, follow a grass path to the top of the slope over two stiles to a single-track tarmac road. Turn left and follow the road (beside the railway) to a farm.

- Just before the farm, turn right up steps to bypass it on a signed grassy path. Afterwards, return to the broad lane and follow it uphill to a stile.

- Follow the grassy track still beside the mainline railway. Although views are now restricted as you pass among gorse bushes and open grassland, easy walking makes for rhythmic progress. Notices tell you about local wildlife from badgers and foxes to peregrine falcons and fulmars.

Burnmouth's harbours at mid-tide

Path runs beside the mainline railway

- About 3 km beyond the farm you make a left/right dogleg towards the coast, but first look across the railway track to see signs for the border. About 80 m later, further signs mark the gate by which you enter England (mile 52·1).
- From here on, in good visibility you may see the inspiring sight of Lindisfarne Castle about 14 miles/23 km to the south-east, with Bamburgh Castle more prominent to its right – 19 miles away.
- Continue on the clifftop path to Marshall Meadows Caravan Park, and pass through it on a tarmac road. Just before the end of the caravans, turn left over a ladder stile to resume the clifftop path which passes above impressive coastal scenery, with sandy beaches, sea arches and caves.
- About 2·5 km after the caravan park, reach Magdalene Fields golf course with caves and sea arches below. The track skirts around the shore side of the golf course and crosses a footbridge to reach Berwick Holiday Park (caravans).
- Take the path to the left around the boundary of Berwick Holiday Park on the shore side. Reach a small car park at the side of a road. The BCP drops down through a timber gate on the left, but you leave it here by taking the road ahead past the golf clubhouse (mile 55·5).
- Bear left past Berwick Bowling Club and after 100 m follow the road as it passes through the Cowport gateway under Berwick's impressive ramparts.
- Turn right across the Parade and its car park to reach St Andrew's Church, which is affiliated to the Church of Scotland, and marks the end of this section.

St Andrew's Church

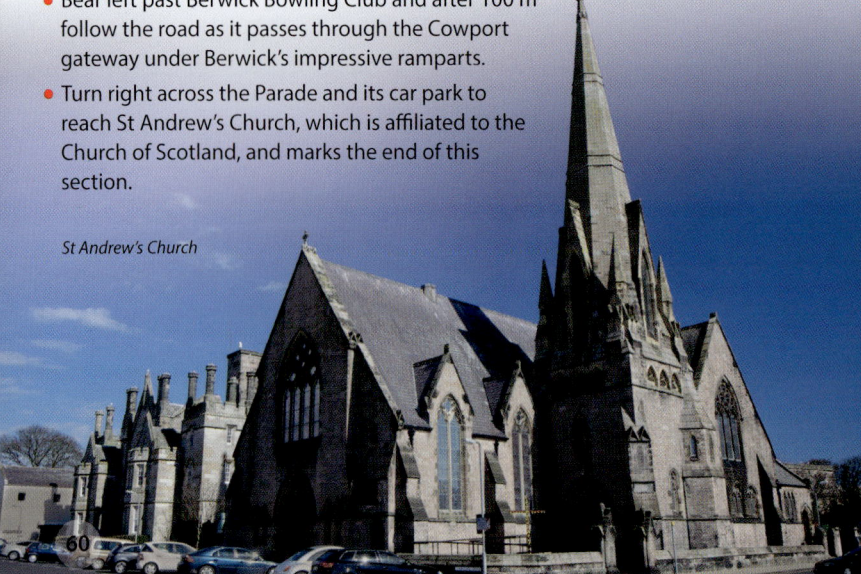

Berwick upon Tweed

England's northernmost town sits mainly on the Scottish side of the Tweed. With a population of 12,000 it is the largest town on the Way. It changed hands 14 times in the two centuries leading up to 1482 when Edward IV captured it. He gave Berwick special status – 'of' the Kingdom of England but not 'in' it. This had the bizarre result that the town remained officially at war with Russia for a century after 1856, because the peace Treaty of Paris failed to mention Berwick.

The old road bridge was completed in 1624 and was the fifth on that site, its predecessors lost to floods and the English. It stands beside the 'new' road bridge completed in 1928. Both are overshadowed by the magnificent 28-arch Royal Border Bridge (1850), which carries the mainline railway.

Your progress from the Cowport clockwise around the ramparts is charted by a series of boards that colour code the defences from medieval times to 18th century. The first section runs around the Elizabethan defences, past the gunpowder magazine and King's Mount. The next section has 18th century defences, including Fisher's Fort where a battery of cannons guarded the mouth of the Tweed. The final section runs on the Quay Walls and down to the river.

Cannon at Fisher's Fort

The medieval walls were built by Edward I in the early 14th century, with some improvements made by Henry VIII in 1539-42. About 1558-60, new walls were built, referred to as Elizabethan. They enclosed only two-thirds of the area bounded by the medieval wall, designed as a military facility, not as protection for the townspeople.

The walls had arrowhead bastions that were later enhanced. These are low irregular polygons projecting from the walls, shaped so that the guns could cover every angle. This was a radical change: in medieval times, high walls were effective, but as artillery improved they offered an easy target. Low fortifications that artillery shells could fly over became more useful.

Berwick's barracks were built after the Jacobite uprising of 1715 and can be visited: see page 70. The town remained under military control until the late 19th century and became part of Northumberland only in 1885. This background explains why Berwick is Britain's finest example of a walled town.

The Way crosses Berwick's old road bridge

Part of the Elizabethan walls

63

3·5 Berwick upon Tweed to Lindisfarne

Distance	**14·0 miles 22·5 km**
Terrain	tarmac roads/pavements, a promenade, grassy paths ending with the sands of the Pilgrim Way
Grade	mainly level
Food and drink	Berwick, Barn at Beal (1·4 km offroute), Lindisfarne village
Side-trip	Lindisfarne Priory, Castle, and Centre
Summary	from Berwick's ramparts and Spittal's promenade, follow the coast and time your approach carefully to reach Lindisfarne by the Pilgrim Way across the sands

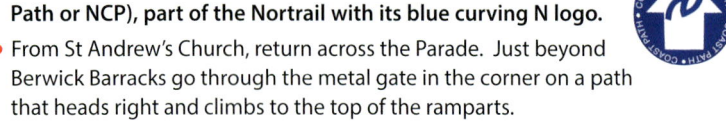

Follow signs for the Coast Path (aka Northumberland Coast Path or NCP), part of the Nortrail with its blue curving N logo.

- From St Andrew's Church, return across the Parade. Just beyond Berwick Barracks go through the metal gate in the corner on a path that heads right and climbs to the top of the ramparts.

- Turn right to follow the fortifications which make a splendid elevated walkway passing clockwise around the town centre: see page 62. After 900 m you swing right along the Quay Walls above the River Tweed.

- Descend to the river and and turn left to cross it by the old road bridge, with fine views of the modern road bridge and the Royal Border (railway) bridge to your right.

- After the bridge turn left (unsigned) into Main Street, Tweedmouth, and after 220 m bear left (unsigned) along Dock Road. Continue for 1·1 km until, after Tweedmouth Town Green and the lifeboat station, it becomes Main Street, Spittal (mile 57·8).

- Within 400 m, pass St John's Church and bear left (unsigned) along South Greenwich Road past a play area to reach Spittal's fine promenade at mile 58·4, with signs for the Lowry Trail paintings.

- After 1 km, near the end of the promenade, take the tarmac path on the right (signed 'public footpath') that climbs the slope diagonally. At the top, follow an NCP fingerpost to turn left along a rough road.

- Continue on the farm road for about 2 km until you pick up a tarmac road at Seahouse (mile 59·8), with a level crossing visible to your right. Turn left past the stone buildings and continue parallel to the coast, at first on a road, later on a restricted byway.

- Turn right at the signboard for Cocklawburn Dunes Nature Reserve at a fingerpost that promises 'Holy Island Causeway 5½ miles'. Immediately turn left on a fenced farm track by squeezing through a gap beside the gates. At mile 61·4, pass a fine fishing pond on your right.

- About 650 m beyond the pond, arrive at Cheswick Sands car park. Here the route makes a tiny detour inland through gates, crossing the road from Cheswick.

- Continue ahead, soon picking up the inland boundary of Goswick Golf Course. Within 850 m of the car park, make a right-left dogleg to go alongside the mainline railway for 500 m.

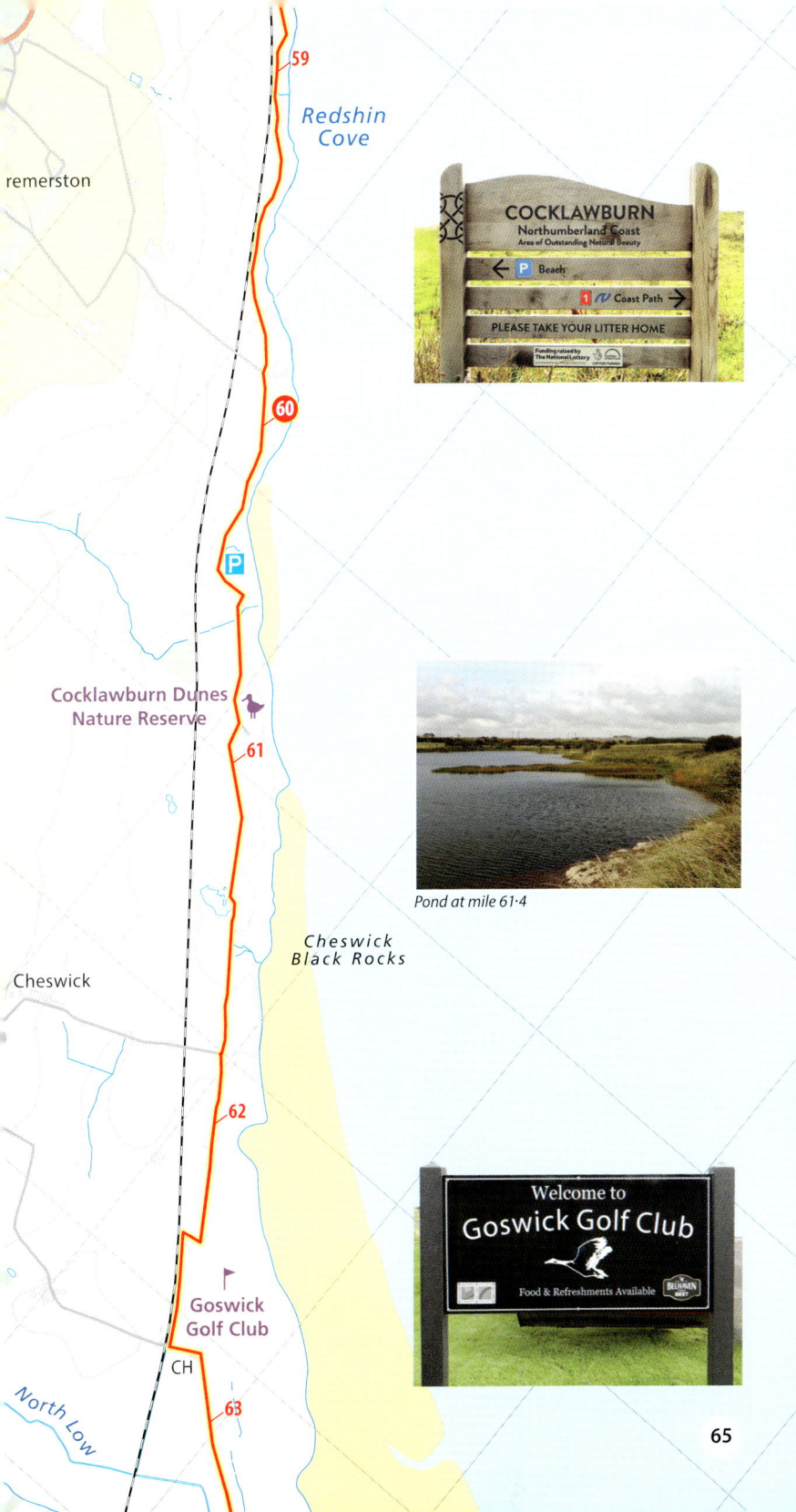

Redshin Cove

Cocklawburn Dunes Nature Reserve

Cheswick Black Rocks

Cheswick

Goswick Golf Club

North Low

Pond at mile 61·4

Footbridge over the South Low River

- At mile 62·7, turn left onto the road to the clubhouse, then turn right past it at a fingerpost. After 900 m, exit the golf club grounds as you cross the North Low River, still on tarmac.
- Pass the buildings at Goswick and continue ahead. After Coastguard Cottage and other houses, the road bends right and its surface gets rougher. Go through a gate onto a narrow field-edge path beside a fence (mile 64·2).
- Follow the path as it bends around the corner of a field and the low causeway becomes visible ahead over the salt marsh and sands, perhaps with toylike cars running across it.
- About mile 65·4, turn right (inland) on an embanked path to the gated footbridge over the South Low River. Once across, leave the cycle route by turning left down timber steps on a narrow, soggy path beside the river.
- After skirting a field, round the rocky outcrop at Beal Point, with the causeway and its refuges now obvious ahead.
- Head for the car park (mile 66·4) and turn left to embark on the causeway, joining two other long walks – St Cuthbert's Way and St Oswald's Way – which also end on the Holy Island of Lindisfarne.

  Before proceeding, check whether tide times are suitable for a safe crossing by your intended route: see panel. Do not embark on the Pilgrim Way on a rising tide. Once the tide is falling, wait for an hour after the causeway opens before setting out across flooded sands.
- If using the Pilgrim Way, leave the causeway after the refuge (with emergency phone) which marks where you re-cross the South Low River.

Causeway refuge at dawn (mile 66·7)

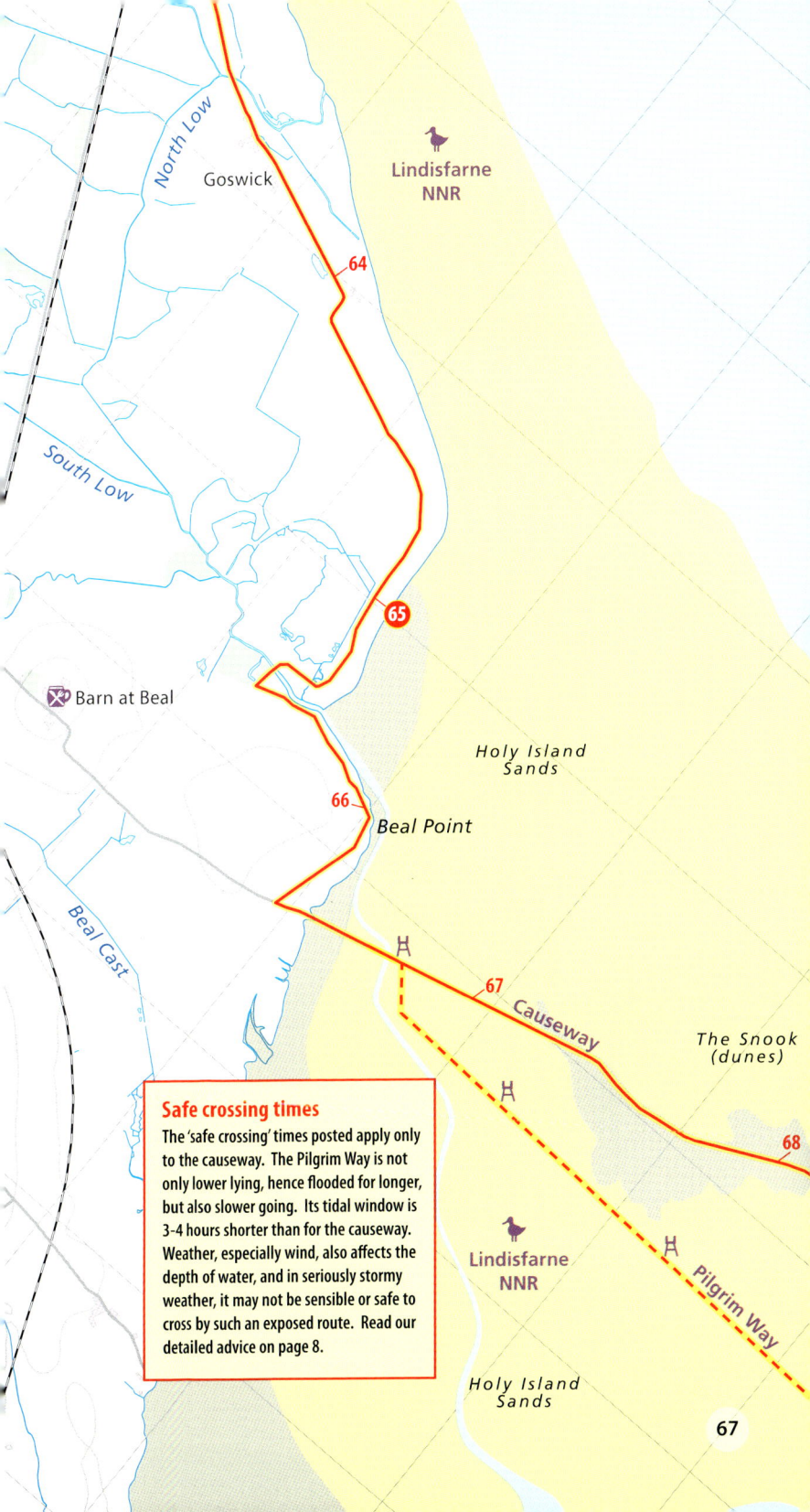

Pilgrim Way refuge and posts

- Then follow the line of timber posts almost due east across the sands for 3·8 km, past the first of two further refuges on stilts. It lacks the luxury of a roof, and its first ladder rung would be quite a stretch: see photo above.
- Otherwise use the road causeway, having checked the tide times for both your outward and return journeys.
- Whichever route you take, once you gain dry land at Lindisfarne, follow the road inland to a car park. The road turns right and you follow Chare Ends to Marygate.
- Make a right-left dogleg into Crossgate Lane, and follow it south to reach Lindisfarne Priory, near the southern tip of Lindisfarne.

Congratulations on completing a long and challenging pilgrim route.

Holy Island of Lindisfarne

Lindisfarne's permanent population is only about 180, but it is swollen massively by daily visitors. Its unique atmosphere is best savoured after the day-trippers have gone home. Once the causeway is flooded by the North Sea, it reverts to a true island and you can immerse yourself in its peace. Until the mid-20th century it was extremely remote, with mains electricity arriving only in 1956 and the causeway in 1966.

In AD 635 St Aidan came from Iona and founded his monastery here, and St Cuthbert later became its third Prior. After eight years as a hermit on the Farne Islands, he returned to Lindisfarne as its bishop in AD 684. The famous Lindisfarne Gospels were inscribed and richly decorated to celebrate his memory in about AD 715-720. The original is confined to the British Library, but you can view its gloriously illustrated pages in the Lindisfarne Centre in both facsimile and digital form.

Visit the Centre, which is run by the Lindisfarne Community Development Trust, on Marygate. It displays not only the Gospels but also explains the Viking raid of AD 793 and the wildlife and ecology: *www.lindisfarnecentre.org*.

The Trust also maintains four sites worth visiting, all free of charge: the old lookout tower (south of the priory), the gospel garden (on Marygate), the old lifeboat house (facing St Cuthbert's Isle) and the Window on Wild Lindisfarne (at the foot of Marygate).

The island's two main visitor attractions are the priory itself (see page 17) and Lindisfarne Castle with its walled garden by Gertrude Jekyll (1911). Built as a fort in 1550, the derelict castle was bought in 1902 by Edward Hudson and restored by Sir Edwin Lutyens. After a £3 million restoration, it was due to reopen in 2021: see page 70.

Wildlife lovers will enjoy excellent sightings of seals, seabirds and (in summer) butterflies. The recommended nature trail starts from the harbour (south coast) and proceeds anticlockwise around the main part of the island, past the Lough where there is a viewing hide. To download its leaflet, and for websites about the island, see page 70.

Top: St Aidan's statue outside the priory
Right: East over Lindisfarne Castle

4 Reference

The Forth to Farne Way was created by a small group interested in early pilgrimage in the ancient Kingdom of Northumbria. The group received support from the Scottish Pilgrim Routes Forum to develop this into the walk that is described online at *forthtofarne.org*. The route was formally launched in October 2017 at Whitekirk by Lord Wilson of Tillyorn.

We thank Community Windpower for financial support through *BeGreen Dunbar* towards the route's development and the publication of this guidebook.

Useful websites

In addition to the SPRF website
forthtofarne.org please visit the publisher's website
rucsacs.com/books/f2f where you will find route updates and other content. Whilst the web links listed below were valid when the book was printed, they are maintained via our website at
rucsacs.com/route-links/f2f

Leaflets can be downloaded from the Edinburgh Geological Society's website:
bit.ly/RR-EGS. Relevant titles include North Berwick Volcanoes, Dunbar Geology Walk, Barns Ness Fossils, Siccar Point and St Abb's Head.

The Way runs along parts of the John Muir Way, the Berwickshire Coastal Path and the Northumberland Coast Path:
johnmuirway.org
bit.ly/RR-BCP
northumberlandcoastpath.org.
For the North Sea Trail (Nortrail), see
northseatrail.org

Historic Environment Scotland is the government agency responsible for Scotland's historic environment, including Dunglass Collegiate Church:
historicenvironment.scot.

English Heritage looks after Lindisfarne Priory and in 2020 visitors had to book timed slots so as to limit visitor numbers:
english-heritage.org.uk. It also cares for Berwick's Barracks and Castle.

The National Trust cares for Lindisfarne Castle, which was due to reopen in 2021:
nationaltrust.org.uk.

Lindisfarne websites

Subject to tides, the Lindisfarne Centre is normally open 7 days per week in season (mid-March to end October) from 10.00 to 16.30. Check its website:
lindisfarnecentre.org.

For causeway safe crossing times, visit the County Council's website
bit.ly/RR-causeway.

Two general websites about the island:
holy-island.com
lindisfarne.org.uk.

Download a leaflet about Lindisfarne's National Nature Reserve, which protects large areas of coast, dunes and the island itself: *bit.ly/RR-Lindis*.

Transport and travel

Check airline sites such as *ba.com*, *easyjet.com*, *ryanair.com*. Edinburgh airport has a wide range of direct flights: *edinburghairport.com*.

For Scottish train services, visit *scotrail.co.uk*. The East Coast mainline is operated by LNER: *lner.co.uk*. For buses, the most relevant services are run by East Coast Buses
bit.ly/RR-eastcoastbuses
Borders Buses
bordersbuses.co.uk
Eve Coaches
eveinfo.co.uk.

Check also Woody's Taxis (tel 01289 547 009) which (pre-Covid) ran a bus service between Beal and Chare Ends and a Castle Shuttle.

For public transport gnerally, try
travelinescotland.com and
traveline.info. For travel from anywhere to anywhere:
Rome2Rio.com.

Further reading

Forth to Farne Way: a pilgrimage in words and pictures (undated) 16 pp, can be downloaded or ordered from
bit.ly/SPRFbooklet

This collection of poems and photos was created by three members of the Forth to Farne Way Steering Group.

The Isle of May Allan, James Allan, Tervor Publishing 4th edition 2015 ISBN 978-0-9538191-2-6; 88 pp
Fascinating stories of the island's geography, history and religious connections, including the priory. As a National Nature Reserve, its wildlife is exceptional.

John Muir Clifftop Trail 2002
Useful 48-pp booklet with foldout map flap which explains the landscape, rock forms and wildlife that John Muir would have known as a boy. No ISBN but available from the John Muir Birthplace in Dunbar's High Street.

The Lindisfarne Gospels Michelle Brown, University of Toronto Press 2003 ISBN 0-8020-8597, 479 pp and CD
Definitive study of one of the world's greatest works of art in book form, by the Curator of Illuminated Manuscripts at the British Library.

Lindisfarne: the cradle island Magnus Magnusson, The History Press, 1984 reprinted 2014 ISBN 978-0-7524-3227-4; 255 pp
Not merely a great and readable book about the island's saints, history and traditions, it is also excellent on the subject of its residents and visitors, human and wildlife.

Maps (printed and online)
Ordnance Survey shows the area of the route on three sheets: 351, 346 and 340. However, it shows the F2F route line only intermittently, and until there is a dedicated route map for the F2F Way, the OS mapping may remain confusing.

For a very detailed online route map, click the map graphic on this page
rucsacs.com/books/f2f and zoom in repeatedly. The page also offers a GPX download (under Bonus content).

Accommodation
Visit these pages for links to accommodation providers:
bit.ly/F2Faccomm
rucsacs.com/route-links/f2f.

Weather forecasts
Forecasts for up to ten days ahead:
metoffice.gov.uk
bbc.co.uk/weather

Notes for novices
If you are new to long-distance walking, read our advice on daily distance, feet and equipment: visit **bit.ly/RR-novices**.

Acknowledgements
We thank Sandra Bardwell for drafting material for Part 2, Dr Roger Crofts for expert advice on geology and the Very Rev Iain Torrance for advice on the reading list. We warmly thank Lindsay Merriman for painstaking proof-reading.

Photo credits
We thank for their images: Ian Capper/**geograph.org.uk** p23u; Cuthbert Centre, Lindisfarne 8; **discovered-light.co.uk** 14; Durham Cathedral p17 mid; Herbert Kratky/**istockphoto.com** p24u; Lynne Kirton p24 mid; Jacquetta Megarry all 95 images not otherwise credited; Martin Peacock p27 (inset butterflies); Jennifer Petrie/
geograph.org.uk p45 mid; Gordon Simm 25 middle two, 26 (godwits); Undiscovered Scotland p17u; Visit Berwickshire Coast front cover; Jim Walker/Eyemouth Museum p21l;

We thank also **dreamstime.com** with the following photographers: Biennguyen title page; Rudmer Zwerver pp4-5; Gail Johnson p15, p17l, p69u; Steve6326 p18; Paul Farnfield p24l; Andreanita p25u; Brian Kushner p25l; Lukas Blazek p26u; Elisa Putti p27u; Whiskybottle p27 (middle two); Chris Moncrieff p39; Sasalan999 p39l; Steve6326 p46l; Tw van Urk p47 & back cover; Toibkk p56u; Dun Liu p60l; Georgesixth p62l, p63; Helen Hotson p66l; Michael Conrad p6u & p69l.

71

Index

A
accommodation 7, 10, 71
altitude profile 10-11

B
bar-tailed godwit 26
Bass Rock 15, 25
Beal 8, 9, 67
Berwick upon Tweed 7, 9, 10, 60, 62, 64
bloody cranesbill 27
Burnmouth 9, 10, 22, 59
bus travel 9, 70
butterflies 24, 27

C
coastal communities 21-23
coastal habitat 25-26
Cockburnspath 10, 43, 45, 46
Coldingham, Coldingham Bay 10, 54, 56
Coldingham Priory 16-17, 56

D
distances and time needed 7-8
dogs 13-14
Dunbar 7, 9, 10, 37, 38, 39
Dunglass Collegiate Church 16, 43, 44

E
East Linton 7, 9, 10, 15, 33
eider duck 26
Eyemouth 7, 9, 10, 20, 21, 22, 57, 58

F
farmland 24
fishing 21

G
gannet 25
geology 18-20
goldcrest 24
Gunsgreen House 58

H
hare, brown 24
Hutton, James 47

I
Isle of May 25, 28, 71

L
lifeboats, RNLI 23
lighthouses 5, 18, 22, 40, 52
Lindisfarne Castle 69, 70
Lindisfarne, Holy Island of 10, 23, 68, 69, 70
Lindisfarne Priory 17, 68, 69, 70

M
maps 12, 71
marram grass 26-7
Mire Loch 19, 24, 51
mobile phones 17
Muir, John 36, 37, 38, 71

N
North Berwick 7, 9, 10, 28, 29
Northern brown argus 27
Notes for novices 5, 71

O
oystercatcher 25

P
packing checklist 14
peregrine falcon 25, 59
Pilgrim Way 8, 66-68
pilgrims, pilgrimage 15-17, 28
planning your walk 5-17
Prestonkirk Parish Church 33
Preston Mill 33

R
redshank 25
refreshments 10
rock rose 27

S
St Abb's Head 19, 51,
St Abbs (village) 10, 21, 22, 52, 53, 54
St Aidan 17, 69
St Baldred 15, 33
St Cuthbert 4, 17, 26, 69
St Ebba (also Abb, Aebba) 16, 53
seal, common and grey 26, 69
smuggling 22, 23, 58

T
terrain 10-11
tide times, tides at Easter 6, 66, 67, 70
Torness power station 40, 42
transport and travel 9, 70

U
Usher, Andrew 16, 52, 53

V
viper's bugloss 27

W
waymarking 12, 29, 39, 46, 54, 64
weather 6, 71
Whitekirk 4, 9, 15, 32
wildflowers and insects 27
wildlife and habitats 24-27